CHRONICLES ABROAD

Cairo

CHRONICLES ABROAD

Cairo

Edited by John and Kirsten Miller

CHRONICLE BOOKS
SAN FRANCISCO

Printed in Hong Kong.

Library of Congress Cataloging-in-Publication Data
Cairo / edited by John and Kirsten Miller.
    p.   cm. — (Chronicles Abroad)
            ISBN 0-8118-0492-5
1. Cairo (Egypt)—Miscellanea. 2. Cairo (Egypt)—
Literary collections. I. Miller, John 1959-
    II. Miller, Kirsten 1962-   III. Series.
    DT143/C28 1994
    808.8'9326216—dc20   93-1815
                                            CIP

Editing and design: Big Fish Books
Composition: Jennifer Petersen, Big Fish Books

Distributed in Canada by Raincoast Books,
112 East Third Avenue, Vancouver, B.C. V5T 1C8

10 9 8 7 6 5 4 3 2 1

Chronicle Books
275 Fifth Street
San Francisco, CA 94103

Contents

Special thanks to Samir Mobayed

and Maggie dePagter

Rudyard Kipling

PREFACE

ONE OF THE MEN told me he thought well of Cairo. It was interesting. "Take it from me," he said, "there's a lot in seeing places, because you can remember 'em afterward."

He was very right. The purple and lemon-coloured hazes of dusk and reflected day spread over the throbbing, twinkling streets, masked the great outline of the citadel and the desert hills, and conspired to confuse and suggest and evoke memories till Cairo the Sorceress cast her proper shape and danced before me in the heart-breaking likeness of every city I had known and loved, a little farther up the road.

English novelist Rudyard Kipling, author of Just So Stories *and* The Jungle Book, *arrived in Cairo and proclaimed it a "kennel."*

Naguib Mahfouz

BLESSED NIGHT

IT WAS NOTHING but a single room in the unpretentious Nouri Alley, off Clot Bey Street. In the middle of the room was the bar and the shelf embellished with bottles. It was called The Flower and was passionately patronized by old men addicted to drink. Its barman was advanced in years, excessively quiet, a man who inspired silence and yet effused a cordial friendliness. Unlike other

---

Naguib Mahfouz was born in Cairo in 1911 and began writing when he was seventeen. Between that time and 1988—when he won the Nobel Prize for Literature—Mahfouz produced over thirty novels, including his masterwork, The Cairo Trilogy. *This 1965 short story is from the collection* The Time and the Place.

taverns, The Flower dozed in a delightful tranquility. The regulars would converse inwardly, with glances rather than words. On the night that was blessed, the barman departed from his traditional silence.

"Yesterday," he said, "I dreamed that a gift would be presented to a man of good fortune. . . . "

Safwan's heart broke into a song with gentle lute accompaniment, while alcoholic waves flowed through him like electricity as he congratulated himself with the words "O blessed, blessed night!" He left the bar, reeling drunk, and plunged into the sublime night under an autumn sky that was not without a twinkling of stars. He made his way toward Nuzha Street, cutting across the square, glowing with an intoxication unadulterated by the least sensation of drowsiness. The street was humbled under the veil of darkness, except for the light from the regularly spaced streetlamps, the shops having closed their doors and given themselves up to sleep. He stood in front of his house: the fourth on the right, Number 42, a single-storied house fronted by an old courtyard of whose garden nothing remained but a solitary towering date palm. Astonished at the dense darkness that surrounded the house, he wondered why his wife had not as usual turned on the light by the front door. It seemed that the house was manifesting itself in a new, gloomily forlorn shape and that it exuded a smell like that of old age. Raising his voice, he called out. "Hey there!"

From behind the fence there rose before his eyes the form of a man, who coughed and inquired, "Who are you? What do you want?"

Safwan was startled at the presence of this stranger and asked sharply, "And who are you? What's brought you to my house?"

"Your house?" said the man in a hoarse, angry voice.

"Who are you?"

"I am the guardian for religious endowment properties."

"But this is my house."

"This house has been deserted for ages," the man

scoffed. "People avoid it because it's rumored to be haunted by spirits."

Safwan decided he must have lost his way, and hurried back toward the square. He gave it a long comprehensive look, then raised his head to the street sign and read out loud, "Nuzha." So again he entered the street and counted off the houses until he arrived at the fourth. There he stood in a state of bewilderment, almost of panic: he could find neither his own house nor the haunted one. Instead he saw an empty space, a stretch of wasteland lying between the other houses. "Is it my house that I've lost or my mind?" he wondered.

He saw a policeman approaching, examining the locks of the shops. He stood in his path and pointed toward the empty wasteland. "What do you see there?"

The policeman stared at him suspiciously and muttered, "As you can see, it's a piece of wasteland where they sometimes set up funeral pavilions."

"That's just where I should have found my house," said Safwan. "I left it there with my wife inside it in the pink of health only this afternoon, so when could it have been pulled down and all the rubble cleared away?"

The policeman concealed an involuntary smile behind a stern official glare and said brusquely, "Ask that deadly poison in your stomach!"

"You are addressing a former general manager," said Safwan haughtily. At this the policeman grasped him by the arm and led him off. "Drunk and disorderly in the public highway!"

He took Safwan to the Daher police station, a short distance away, where he was brought before the officer on a charge of being drunk and disorderly. The officer took pity on him, however, because of his age and his respectable appearance. "Your identity card?"

Safwan produced it and said, "I'm quite in my right mind, it's just that there's no trace of my house."

"Well, now there's a new type of theft!" said the officer, laughing. "I really don't believe it!"

"But I'm speaking the truth," said Safwan in alarm.

"The truth's being unfairly treated, but I'll be

lenient in deference to your age." Then he said to the policeman, "Take him to Number 42 Nuzha Street."

Accompanied by the policeman, Safwan finally found himself in front of his house as he knew it. Despite his drunken state he was overcome with confusion. He opened the outer door, crossed the courtyard, and put on the light at the entrance, where he was immediately taken aback, for he found himself in an entrance he had never before set eyes on. There was absolutely no connection between it and the entrance of the house in which he had lived for about half a century, and whose furniture and walls were all in a state of decay. He decided to retreat before his mistake was revealed, so he darted into the street, where he stood scrutinizing the house from the outside. It was his house all right, from the point of view of its features and site, and he had opened the door with his own key, no doubt about it. What, then, had changed the inside? He had seen a small chandelier, and the walls had been papered. There was also a new carpet. In a way it was his house, and in another way it was not. And what about his wife, Sadriyya? "I've been drinking for half a century," he said aloud, "so what is it about this blessed night?"

He imagined his seven married daughters looking at him with tearful eyes. He determined, though, to solve the problem by himself, without recourse to the authorities—which would certainly mean exposing himself to the wrath of the law. Going up to the fence, he began clapping his hands, at which the front door was opened by someone whose features he could not make out. A woman's voice could be heard asking, "What's keeping you outside?"

It seemed, though he could not be certain, that it was the voice of a stranger. "Whose house is this, please?" he inquired.

"Are you that drunk? It's just too much!"

"I'm Safwan," he said cautiously.

"Come in or you'll wake the people sleeping."

"Are you Sadriyya?"

"Heaven help us! There's someone waiting for you inside."

"At this hour?"

"He's been waiting since ten."

"Waiting for me?"

She mumbled loudly in exasperation, and he inquired again, "Are you Sadriyya?"

Her patience at an end, she shouted, "Heaven help us!"

He advanced, at first stealthily, then without caring, and found himself in the new entrance. He saw that the door of the sitting room was open, with the lights brightly illuminating the interior. As for the woman, she had disappeared. He entered the sitting room, which revealed itself to him in a new garb, as the entrance had. Where had the old room with its ancient furniture gone to? Walls recently painted and a large chandelier from which Spanish-style lamps hung, a blue carpet, a spacious sofa and armchairs: it was a splendid room. In the foreground sat a man he had not seen before: thin, of a dark brown complexion, with a nose reminding one of a parrot's beak, and a certain impetuosity in the eyes. He was wearing a black suit, although autumn was only just coming in. The man addressed him irritably. "How late you are for our appointment!"

Safwan was both taken aback and angry. "What appointment? Who are you?"

"That's just what I expected—you'd forgotten!" the man exclaimed. "It's the same old complaint repeated every single day, whether it's the truth or not. It's no use, it's out of the question. . . . "

"What is this raving nonsense?" Safwan shouted in exasperation.

Restraining himself, the man said, "I know you're a man who enjoys his drink and sometimes overdoes it."

"You're speaking to me as though you were in charge of me, while I don't even know you. I'm amazed you should impose your presence on a house in the absence of its owner."

He gave a chilly smile. "It's owner?"

"As though you doubt it!" Safwan said vehemently. "I see I'll have to call the police."

"So they can arrest you for being drunk and disorderly—and for fraud?"

"Shut up—you insolent imposter!"

The man struck one palm against the other and said, "You're pretending not to know who I am so as to escape from your commitments. It's out of the question . . . "

"I don't know you and I don't know what you're talking about."

"Really? Are you alleging you forgot and are therefore innocent? Didn't you agree to sell your house and wife and fix tonight for completing the final formalities?"

Safwan, in a daze, exclaimed, "What a lying devil you are!"

"As usual. You're all the same—shame on you!" said the other, with a shrug of the shoulders.

"You're clearly mad."

"I have the proof and witnesses."

"I've never heard of anyone having done such a thing before."

"But it happens every moment. You're putting on a good act, even though you're drunk."

In extreme agitation, Safwan said, "I demand you leave at once."

"No, let's conclude the incompleted formalities," said the other in a voice full of confidence.

He got up and went toward the closed door that led to the interior of the house. He rapped on it, then returned to his seat. Immediately there entered a short man with a pug nose and prominent forehead, carrying under his arm a file stuffed with papers. He bowed in greeting and sat down. Safwan directed a venomous glare at him and exclaimed, "Since when has my house become a shelter for the homeless?"

The first man, introducing the person who had just entered, said, "The lawyer."

At which Safwan asked him brusquely, "And who gave you permission to enter my house?"

"You're in a bad way," said the lawyer, smiling, "but may God forgive you. What are you so angry about?"

"What insolence!"

Without paying any attention to what Safwan had said, the lawyer went on. "The deal is undoubtedly to your advantage."

"What deal?" asked Safwan in bewilderment.

"You know exactly what I mean, and I would like to tell you that it's useless your thinking of going back on it now. The law is on our side, and common sense too. Let me ask you: Do you consider this house to be really yours?"

For the first time Safwan felt at a loss. "Yes and no," he said.

"Was it in this condition when you left it?"

"Not at all."

"Then it's another house?"

"Yet it's the same site, number, and street."

"Ah, those are fortuitous incidentals that don't affect the essential fact—and there's something else."

He got up, rapped on the door, and returned to his seat. All at once a beautiful middle-aged woman, well dressed and with a mournful mien, entered and seated herself alongside the first man. The lawyer resumed his questioning. "Do you recognize in this lady your wife?"

It seemed to Safwan that she did possess a certain

similarity, but he could not stop himself from saying, "Not at all."

"Fine—the house is neither your house, nor the lady your wife. Thus nothing remains but for you to sign the final agreement and then you can be off. . . . "

"Off! Where to?"

"My dear sir, don't be stubborn. The deal is wholly to your advantage, and you know it."

The telephone rang, although it was very late at night. The caller was the barman. Safwan was astonished that the man should be telephoning him for the first time in his life. "Safwan Bey," he said, "Sign without delay."

"But do you know. . . . "

"Sign. It's the chance of a lifetime."

The receiver was replaced at the other end. Safwan considered the short conversation and found himself relaxing. In a second his state of mind changed utterly, his face took on a cheerful expression, and a sensation of calm spread throughout his body. The feeling of tension left him, and he signed. When he had done so, the lawyer handed him a small but somewhat heavy suitcase and said, "May the Almighty bless your comings and goings. In this suitcase is all that a happy man needs in this world."

The first man clapped, and there entered an extremely portly man, with a wide smile and a charming manner. Introducing him to Safwan, the lawyer said, "This is a trustworthy man and an expert at his work. He will take you to your new abode. It is truly a profitable deal."

The portly man made his way outside, and Safwan followed him, quiet and calm, his hand gripping the handle of the suitcase. The man walked ahead of him into the night, and Safwan followed. Affected by the fresh air, he staggered and realized that he had not recovered from the intoxication of the blessed night. The man quickened his pace, and the distance between them grew, so Safwan in turn, despite his drunken state, walked faster, his gaze directed toward the specter of the other man, while wondering how it was that he combined such agility with portliness. "Take it easy, sir!" Safwan called out to him.

But it was as though he had spurred the man on

to greater speed, for he broke into strides so rapid that Safwan was forced to hurl himself forward for fear he would lose him, and thus lose his last hope. Frightened he could be incapable of keeping up the pace, he once again called out to the man. "Take it easy or I'll get lost!"

At this the other, unconcerned about Safwan, began to run. Safwan, in terror, raced ahead, heedless of the consequences. This caused him great distress, but all to no avail, for the man plunged into the darkness and disappeared from sight. Safwan was frightened the man would arrive ahead of him at Yanabi Square, where various roads split up, and he would not know which one the man had taken. He therefore began running as fast as possible, determined to catch up.

His efforts paid off, for once again he caught a glimpse of the specter of the man at the crossroads. He saw him darting forward toward the fields, ignoring the branch roads that turned off to the eastern and western parts of the city. Safwan hurried along behind him and continued running without stopping, and without the least feeling of weakness. His nostrils were filled with delightful aromas that stirred up all kinds of sensations he had never before properly experienced and enjoyed. .

When the two of them were alone in the vast void of earth and sky, the portly man gradually began to slow down until he had reverted to a mere brisk trot, then to a walk. Finally he stopped, and Safwan caught up with him and also came to a breathless stop. He looked around at the all-pervading darkness, with the glittering lights of faint stars. "Where's the new abode?" he asked.

The man maintained his silence. At the same time, Safwan began to feel the incursion of a new weight bearing down upon his shoulders and his whole body. The weight grew heavier and heavier and then rose upward to his head. It seemed to him that his feet would plunge deep into the ground. The pressure became so great that he could no longer bear it and, with a sudden spontaneous burst of energy, he took off his shoes. Then, the pressure working its way upward, he stripped himself of his jacket and trousers and flung them to the ground. This made no real difference, so he rid himself of his underclothes, heedless of the dampness of autumn. He was ablaze with pain and, groaning, he abandoned the suitcase on the ground. At that moment it seemed to him that he had regained his balance, that he was capable of taking the few steps that still remained. He waited for his companion to do something, but the man was sunk in silence. Safwan wanted to converse with him, but talk was impossible, and the overwhelming silence slipped through the pores of his skin to his very heart. It seemed that in a little while he would be hearing the conversation that was passing between the stars.

Alexandre Kinglake

CAIRO AND THE PLAGUE

CAIRO AND PLAGUE! During the whole time of my stay the Plague was so master of the city, and stared so plain in every street and every alley, that I can't now affect to dissociate the two ideas.

When, coming from the Desert, I rode through a village lying near to the city on the eastern side, there approached me with busy face and earnest gestures a person-

---

Victorian gentleman and novelist Alexandre Kinglake set out for the wilds of the Sahara in 1834. His journal, Eothen: Traces of Travel Brought Home from the East, *was originally published anonymously. The best-selling volume was traced to the writer, who was promptly dubbed "Eothen" Kinglake.*

age in the Turkish dress; his long flowing beard gave him rather a majestic look, but his briskness of manner and his visible anxiety to accost me seemed strange in an Oriental. The man in fact was French or of French origin, and his object was to warn me of the Plague, and prevent me from entering the city.

Arrêtez-vous, Monsieur, je vous en prie—arrêtez-vous; il ne faut pas entrer dans la ville; la Peste y règne partout.

Oui, je sais, mais—

Mais, Monsieur, je dis la Peste—la Peste; c'est de LA PESTE qu'il est question.

Oui, je sais, mais—

Mais, Monsieur, je dis encore LA PESTE—LA PESTE. Je vous conjure de ne pas entrer dans la ville—vous seriez dans une ville empestée.

Oui, je sais, mais—

Mais, Monsieur, je dois donc vous avertir tout bonnement que si vous entrez dans la ville, vous serez—enfin vous serez COMPROMIS!

Oui, je sais, mais—

The Frenchman was at last convinced that it was vain to reason with a mere Englishman who could not understand what it was to be "compromised." I thanked him most sincerely for his kindly meant warning. In hot countries it is very unusual indeed for a man to go out in the glare of the sun and give free advice to a stranger.

When I arrived at Cairo I summoned Osman Effendi, who was, as I knew, the owner of several houses, and would be able to provide me with apartments; he had no difficulty in doing this, for there was not one European traveller in Cairo besides myself. Poor Osman! he met me with a sorrowful countenance, for the fear of the Plague sat heavily on his soul; he seemed as if he felt that he was doing wrong in lending me a resting-place, and he betrayed such a listlessness about temporal matters as one might look for in a man who believed that his days were numbered. He caught me, too, soon after my arrival, coming out from the public baths, and from that time forward he was sadly afraid of me, for upon the subject of contagion he held European opinions.

Osman's history is a curious one. He was a Scotchman born, and when very young, being then a drummer-boy, he landed in Egypt with Fraser's force. He was taken prisoner, and according to Mahometan custom, the alternative of Death or the Koran was offered to him; he did not choose Death, and therefore went through the ceremonies necessary for turning him into a good Mahometan. But what amused me most in his history was this—that very soon after having embraced Islam, he was obliged in practice to become curious and discriminating in his new faith—to make war upon Mahometan dissenters, and follow the orthodox standard of the Prophet in fierce campaigns against the Wahabees, the Unitarians of the Mussulman world. The Wahabees were crushed, and Osman, returning home in triumph from his holy wars, began to flourish in the world; he acquired property, and became effendi, or gentleman. At the time of my visit to Cairo he seemed to be much respected by his brother Mahometans, and gave pledge of his sincere alienation from Christianity by keeping a couple of wives. He affected the same sort of reserve in mentioning them as is generally shown by Orientals. He invited me, indeed, to see his Hareem, but he made both his wives bundle out before I was admitted; he felt, as it seemed to me, that neither of them would bear criticism, and I think that this idea, rather than any motive of sincere jealousy, induced him to keep them out of sight. The rooms of the hareem reminded me of an English nursery, rather than of a Mahometan paradise. One is apt to judge of a woman before one sees her by the air of elegance or coarseness with which she surrounds her home: I judged Osman's wives by this test, and condemned them both. But the strangest feature in Osman's character was his inextinguishable nationality. In vain they had brought him over the seas in early boyhood—in vain had he suffered captivity, conversion, circumcision—in vain they had passed him through fire in their Arabian campaigns—they could not cut away or burn out poor Osman's inborn love of all that was Scotch; in vain men called him Effendi—in vain he swept along in eastern robes—in vain the rival wives adorned his hareem; the joy of his heart still plainly lay in this, that he had three shelves of books, and that the books were thoroughbred Scotch—the Edinburgh this, the Edinburgh that, and above all, I recollect he prided himself upon the "Edinburgh Cabinet Library."

The fear of the Plague is its forerunner. It is likely enough that at the time of my seeing poor Osman the deadly taint was beginning to creep through his veins, but it was not till after I had left Cairo that he was visibly stricken. He died.

As soon as I had seen all that interested me in Cairo and its neighbourhood, I wished to make my escape from a city that lay under the terrible curse of the Plague, but Mysseri fell ill in consequence, I believe, of the hardships which he had been suffering in my service; after a while he recovered sufficiently to undertake a journey, but then there was some difficulty in procuring beasts of burthen, and it was not till the nineteenth day of my sojourn that I quitted the city.

During all this time the power of the Plague was rapidly increasing. When I first arrived, it was said that the daily number of "accidents" by Plague out of a popu-

lation of about 200,000 did not exceed four or five hundred, but before I went away the deaths were reckoned at
twelve hundred a day. I had no means of knowing
whether the numbers (given out, as I believe they were, by
officials) were at all correct, but I could not help knowing
that from day to day the number of the dead was increasing.
My quarters were in one of the chief thoroughfares of the
city, and as the funerals in Cairo take place between day-
break and noon (a time during which I generally stayed in
my rooms), I could form some opinion as to the briskness
of the Plague. I don't mean that I got up every morning
with the sun. It was not so, but the funerals of most people
in decent circumstances at Cairo are attended by singers and
howlers, and the performances of these people woke me in
the early morning and prevented me from remaining in
ignorance of what was going on in the street below.

These funerals were very simply conducted. The
bier was a shallow wooden tray carried upon a light and
weak wooden frame. The tray had in general no lid, but the
body was more or less hidden from view by a shawl or

scarf. The whole was borne upon the shoulders of men, and hurried forward at a great pace. Two or three singers generally preceded the bier; the howlers (these are paid for their vocal labours) followed after; and last of all came such of the dead man's friends and relations as could keep up with such a rapid procession; these, especially the women, would get terribly blown, and would straggle back into the rear; many were fairly "beaten off." I never observed any appearance of mourning in the mourners; the pace was too severe for any solemn affectation of grief.

When first I arrived at Cairo the funerals that daily passed under my windows were many, but still there were frequent and long intervals without a single howl. Every day, however (except one, when I fancied that I observed a diminution of funerals), these intervals became less frequent and shorter, and at last, the passing of the howlers from morn to noon was almost incessant. I believe that about one half of the whole people was carried off by this visitation. The Orientals, however, have more quiet fortitude than Europeans under afflictions of this sort, and they never allow the Plague to interfere with their religious usages. I rode one day round the great burial-ground. The tombs are strewn over a great expanse among the vast mountains of rubbish (the accumulations of many centuries) which surround the city. The ground, unlike the Turkish "cities of the dead," which are made so beautiful by their dark cypresses, has nothing to sweeten melancholy—nothing to mitigate the hatefulness of death. Carnivorous beasts and birds possess the place by night, and now in the fair morning it was all alive with fresh comers—alive with dead. Yet at this very time when the Plague was raging so furiously, and on this very ground which resounded so mournfully with the howls of arriving funerals, preparations were going on for the religious festival called the Kourban Bairam. Tents were pitched, and *swings hung for the amusement of children*—a ghastly holiday! but the Mahometans take a pride, and a just pride, in following their ancient customs undisturbed by the shadow of death.

I did not hear whilst I was at Cairo that any prayer for a remission of the Plague had been offered up in the mosques. I believe that, however frightful the ravages of the disease may be, the Mahometans refrain from approaching Heaven with their complaints until the Plague has endured for a long space, and then at last they pray God—not that the Plague may cease, but that it may go to another city!

A good Mussulman seems to take pride in repudiating the European notion that the will of God can be eluded by shunning the touch of a sleeve. When I went to see the Pyramids of Sakkara, I was the guest of a noble old fellow—an Osmanlee (how sweet it was to hear his soft rolling language, after suffering as I had suffered of late from the shrieking tongue of the Arabs!). This man was aware of the European ideas about contagion, and his first care therefore was to assure me that not a single instance of Plague had occurred in his village; he then inquired as to the progress of the Plague at Cairo. I had but a bad account to give. Up to this time my host had carefully refrained from touching me, out of respect to the European theory of contagion, but as soon as it was made plain that he, and not I, would be the person endangered by contact, he gently laid his hand upon my arm in order to make me feel sure that the circumstances of my coming from an infected city did not occasion him the least uneasiness. In that touch there was true hospitality.

Very different is the faith and the practice of the Europeans, or rather I mean of the Europeans settled in the East, and commonly called Levantines. When I came to the end of my journey over the desert I had been so long alone that the prospect of speaking to somebody at Cairo seemed almost a new excitement. I felt a sort of consciousness that I had a little of the wild beast about me, but I was quite in the humour to be charmingly tame and to be quite engaging in my manners, if I should have an opportunity of holding communion with any of the human race whilst at Cairo. I knew no one in the place, and had no letters of introduction, but I carried letters of credit; and it often happens in places remote from England that those "advices" operate as a sort of introduction, and obtain for the bearer (if disposed to receive them) such ordinary civilities as it may be in the power of the banker to offer.

Very soon after my arrival I found out the abode

of the Levantine to whom my credentials were addressed. At his door several persons (all Arabs) were hanging about and keeping guard. It was not till after some delay and the interchange of some communications with those in the interior of the citadel that I was admitted. At length, however, I was conducted through the court, and up a flight of stairs, and finally into the apartment where business was transacted. The room was divided by a good substantial fence of iron bars, and behind these defences the banker had his station. The truth was that from fear of the Plague he had adopted the course usually taken by European residents, and had shut himself up "in strict quarantine,"—that is to say, that he had, as he hoped, cut himself off from all communication with infecting substances. The Europeans long resident in the East, without any, or with scarcely any exception, are firmly convinced that the Plague is propagated by contact, and by contact only—that if they can but avoid the touch of an infecting substance, they are safe, and that if they cannot, they die. This belief induces them to adopt the contrivance of putting themselves in that state of siege which they call "Quarantine." It is a part of their faith that metals and hempen rope, and also, I fancy, one or two other substances, will not carry the infection: and they likewise believe that the germ of pestilence lying in an infected substance may be destroyed by submersion in water, or by the action of smoke. They, therefore, guard the doors of their houses with the utmost care against intrusion, and condemn themselves with all the members of their family, including European servants, to a strict imprisonment within the walls of their dwelling. Their native attendants are not allowed to enter at all, but they make the necessary purchases of provisions: these are hauled up through one of the windows by means of a rope, and are afterwards soaked in water.

I knew nothing of these mysteries, and was not therefore prepared for the sort of reception I met with. I advanced to the iron fence, and putting my letter between the bars, politely proffered it to Mr. Banker. Mr. Banker received me˙ with a sad and dejected look, and not "with open arms," or with any arms at all, but with—a pair of tongs! I placed my letter between the iron fingers: these instantly picked it up as it were a viper, and conveyed it away to be scorched and purified by fire and smoke. I was disgusted at this reception, and at the idea that any thing of mine could carry infection to the poor wretch who stood on the other side of the bars—pale and trembling, and already meet for Death. I looked with something of the Mahometan's feeling upon these little contrivances for eluding Fate: and in this instance at least they were vain: a little while and the poor money-changer who had strived to guard the days of his life (as though they were coins) with bolts and bars of iron—he was seized by the Plague, and he died.

To people entertaining such opinions as these respecting the fatal effect of contact, the narrow and crowded streets of Cairo were terrible as the easy slope that leads to Avernus. The roaring Ocean and the beetling crags owe something of their sublimity to this—that if they be tempted, they can take the warm life of a man. To the contagionist, filled as he is with the dread of final causes, having no faith in Destiny, nor in the fixed will of

God, and with none of the devil-may-care indifference which might stand him instead of creeds—to such one, every rag that shivers in the breeze of a plague-stricken city has this sort of sublimity. If by any terrible ordinance he be forced to venture forth, he sees Death dangling from every sleeve; and as he creeps forward, he poises his shuddering limbs between the imminent jacket that is stabbing at his right elbow, and the murderous pelisse, that threatens to mow him clean down as it sweeps along on his left. But most of all he dreads that which most of all he should love—the touch of a woman's dress; for mothers and wives hurrying forth on kindly errands from the bedsides of the dying go slouching along through the streets more wilfully and less courteously than the men. For a while it may be that the caution of the poor Levantine may enable him to avoid contact, but sooner or later perhaps the dreaded chance arrives: that bundle of linen, with the dark tearful eyes at the top of it that labours along with the voluptuous clumsiness of Grisi—she has touched the poor Levantine with the hem of her sleeve! From that dread moment, his peace is gone; his mind, for ever hanging upon the fatal touch, invites the blow which he fears; he watches for the symptoms of plague so carefully that sooner or later they come in truth. The parched mouth is a sign—his mouth *is* parched; the throbbing brain—his brain *does* throb; the rapid pulse—he touches his own wrist (for he dares not ask counsel of any man, lest he be deserted), he touches his wrist, and feels how his frighted blood goes galloping out of his heart. There is nothing but the fatal swelling that is wanting to make his sad conviction complete; immediately he has an odd feel under the arm—no pain, but a little straining of the skin; he would to God it were his fancy that were strong enough to give him that sensation: this is the worst of all. It now seems to him that he could be happy and contented with his parched mouth, and his throbbing brain, and his rapid pulse, if only he could know that there were no swelling under the left arm; but dares he try?—in a moment of calmness and deliberation he dares not, but when for a while he has writhed under the torture of suspense, a sudden strength of will drives him to seek and know his fate; he touches the gland, and finds the skin sane and sound, but under the cuticle there lies a small lump like a pistol bullet, that moves as he pushes it. Oh! but is this for all certainty, is this the sentence of death? Feel the gland of the other arm: there is not the same lump exactly, yet something a little like it: have not some people glands naturally enlarged?——would to Heaven he were one! So he does for himself the work of the Plague, and when the Angel of Death thus courted does indeed and in truth come, he has only to finish that which has been so well begun; he passes his fiery hand over the brain of the victim, and lets him rave for a season, but all chance-wise, of people and things once dear, or of people and things indifferent. Once more the poor fellow is back at his home in fair Provence, and sees the sun-dial that stood in his childhood's garden——sees part of his mother, and the long-since-forgotten face of that little dear sister——(he sees her, he says, on a Sunday morning, for all the church bells are ringing;) he looks up and down through the universe and owns it well piled with bales upon bales of cotton and cotton eternal——so much so, that he feels——he knows——he swears he could make that winning hazard, if the billiard table would not slant upwards, and if the cue were a cue worth playing with; but it is not—it's a cue that won't move—his own arm won't move—in short, there's the devil to pay in the brain of the poor Levantine, and, perhaps, the next night but one he becomes the "life and the soul" of some squalling jackal family who fish him out by the foot from his shallow and sandy grave.

Better fate was mine: by some happy perverseness (occasioned perhaps by my disgust at the notion of being received with a pair of tongs) I took it into my pleasant head that all the European notions about contagion were thoroughly unfounded,—that the Plague might be providential, or "epidemic" (as they phrase it), but was not contagious, and that I could not be killed by the touch of a woman's sleeve, nor yet by her blessed breath. I therefore determined that the Plague should not alter my habits and amusements in any one respect. Though I came to this resolve from impulse, I think that I took the course which was in effect the most prudent, for the cheerfulness of spirits which I was thus enabled to retain discouraged the yellow-winged Angel, and prevented him from taking a shot at me. I, however, so far respected the opinion of the Europeans that I avoided touching when I could do so without privation or inconvenience. This endeavour furnished me with a sort of amusement as I passed through the streets. The usual mode of moving from place to place in the city of Cairo is upon donkeys; of these great number are always in readiness with donkey-boys attached. I had two who constantly (until one of them died of the Plague) waited at my door upon the chance of being wanted. I found this way of moving about exceedingly pleasant, and never attempted any other. I had only to mount my beast, and tell my donkey-boy the point for which I was bound, and instantly I began to glide on at a capital pace. The streets of Cairo are not paved in any way, but strewed with a dry sandy soil so deadening to sound, that the foot-fall of my donkey could scarcely be heard. There is no trottoir, and as you ride through the streets, you mingle with the people on foot: those who are in your way upon being warned by the shouts of the donkey-boy move very slightly aside so as to leave you a narrow lane for your passage. Through this you move at a gallop, gliding on delightfully in the very midst of crowds without being inconvenienced or stopped for a moment; it seems to you that it is not the donkey, but the donkey-boy who wafts you along with his shouts through pleasant groups and air that comes thick with the fragrance of burial spice. "Eh! Sheik, Eh! Bint,—reggalek,—shumalek, &c., &c.,—O old man, O virgin, get out of the way on the right—O virgin, O old man get out of the way on the left,—this Englishman comes, he comes, he comes!" The narrow alley which these shouts cleared for my passage made it possible, though difficult, to go on for a long way without touching a single person, and my endeavours to avoid such contact were a sort of game for me in my loneliness. If I got through a street without being touched, I won; if I was touched, I lost,—lost a deuce of a stake according to the theory of the Europeans, but that I deemed to be all nonsense,—I only lost that game, and would certainly win the next.

There is not much in the way of public buildings

to admire in Cairo, but I saw one handsome mosque, and to this an instructive history is attached. A Hindostanee merchant, having amassed an immense fortune, settled in Cairo, and soon found that his riches in the then state of the political world gave him vast power in the city— power, however, the exercise of which was much restrained by the counteracting influence of other wealthy men. With a view to extinguish every attempt at rivalry, the Hindostanee merchant built this magnificent mosque at his own expense; when the work was complete, he invited all the leading men of the city to join him in prayer within the walls of the newly-built temple, and he then caused to be massacred all those who were sufficiently influential to cause him any jealousy or uneasiness,—in short, all "the respectable men" of the place; after this he possessed undisputed power in the city, and was greatly revered,— he is revered to this day. It struck me that there was a touching simplicity in the mode which this man so success- fully adopted for gaining the confidence and good will of his fellow-citizens. There seems to be some improbability in the story (though not nearly so gross as it might appear to an European ignorant of the East, for witness Mehemet Ali's destruction of the Mamelukes, a closely similar act, and attended with the like brilliant success); but even if the story be false as a mere fact, it is perfectly true as an illustration,—it is a true exposition of the means by which the respect and affection of Orientals may be conciliated.

I ascended one day to the citadel, and gained from its ramparts a superb view of the town. The fanciful and elaborate gilt work of the many minarets gives a light, a florid grace to the city as seen from this height; but before you can look for many seconds at such things, your eyes are drawn westward—drawn westward and over the Nile till they rest upon the massive enormities of the Ghizeh pyramids.

I saw within the fortress many yoke of men all haggard and woe-begone, and a kennel of very fine lions well fed and flourishing; I say *yoke* of men, for the poor fellows were working together in bonds; I say a *kennel* of lions, for the beasts were not enclosed in cages, but simply chained up like dogs.

I went round the Bazaars: it seemed to me that pipes and arms were cheaper here than at Constantinople, and I should advise you therefore, if you reach both places, to prefer the market of Cairo. In the open slave-market I saw about fifty girls exposed for sale, but all of them black or "invisible" brown. A slave agent took me to some rooms in the upper story of the building, and also into several obscure houses in the neighbourhood with a view to show me some white women. The owners raised various objections to the display of their ware, and well they might, for I had not the least notion of purchasing: some refused on account of the illegality of selling to unbelievers, and others declared that all transactions of this sort were completely out of the question as long as the Plague was raging. I only succeeded in seeing one white slave who was for sale, but on this treasure the owner affected to set an immense value, and raised my expectations to a high pitch by saying that the girl was Circassian and was "fair as the full moon." There was a good deal of delay, but at last I was led into a long dreary room, and there, after marching timidly forward for a few paces, I descried at the farther end that mass of white linen which indicates an Eastern woman. She was bid to uncover her face, and I presently saw that, though very far from being good looking, according to my notion of beauty, she had not been inaptly described by the man who compared her to the full moon, for her large face was perfectly round, and perfectly white. Though very young, she was neverthe-less extremely fat. She gave me the idea of having been got up for sale,—of having been fattened, and whitened by medicines or by some peculiar diet. I was firmly determined not to see any more of her than the face. She was perhaps disgusted at this my virtuous resolve, as well as with my personal appearance,—perhaps she saw my distaste and dis-appointment; perhaps she wished to gain favour with her owner by showing her attachment to his faith: at all events she holloed out very lustily and very decidedly that "she would not be bought by the Infidel."

Whilst I remained in Cairo, I thought it worth

while to see something of the Magicians, because I considered that these men were in some sort the descendants of those who contended so stoutly against the superior power of Aaron. I therefore sent for an old man who was held to be the chief of the Magicians, and desired him to show me the wonders of his art. The old man looked and dressed his character exceedingly well; the vast turban, the flowing beard, and the ample robes were all that one could wish in the way of appearance. The first experiment (a very stale one) which he attempted to perform for me was that of showing the forms and faces of my absent friends, not to me, but to a boy brought in from the streets for the purpose, and said to be chosen at random. A mangale (pan of burning charcoal) was brought into my room, and the Magician bending over it, sprinkled upon the fire some substances consisting, I suppose, of spices or sweetly burning woods; for immediately a fragrant smoke arose that curled around the bending form of the Wizard, the while that he pronounced his first incantations. When these were over, the boy was made to sit down, and a common green shade was bound over his brow; then the Wizard took ink, and, still continuing his incantations, wrote certain mysterious figures upon the boy's palm and directed him to rivet his attention to these marks without looking aside for an instant. Again the incantations proceeded, and after a while the boy, being seemingly a little agitated, was asked whether he saw anything on the palm of his hand. He declared that he saw, and he described it rather minutely, a kind of military procession with royal flags, and warlike banners flying. I was then called upon to name the absent person whose form was to be made visible. I named Keate. You were not at Eton, and I must tell you, therefore, what manner of man it was that I named, though I think you must have some idea of him already, for wherever from utmost Canada to Bundelcund—wherever there was the white-washed wall of an officer's room or of any other apartment in which English gentlemen are forced to kick their heels, there, likely enough (in the days of his reign) the head of Keate would be seen, scratched, or drawn with those various degrees of skill which one observes in the representation of Saints. Anybody without the least notion of drawing

could still draw a speaking, nay scolding likeness of Keate. If
you had no pencil, you could draw him well enough with a
poker, or the leg of a chair, or the smoke of a candle. He
was little more (if more at all) than five feet in height, and
was not very great in girth, but within this space was concen-
trated the pluck of ten battalions. He had a really noble
voice, and this he could modulate with great skill, but he had
also the power of quacking like an angry duck, and he
almost always adopted this mode of communication in order
to inspire respect. He was a capital scholar, but his ingenuous
learning had *not* "softened his manners," and *had* "permitted
them to be fierce"——tremendously fierce; he had such a complete command over his temper——I mean, over his *good* temper, that he scarcely ever allowed it to appear: you could not
put him out of humour——that is, out of the *ill*-humour
which he thought to be fitting for a head master. His red,
shaggy eyebrows were so prominent, that he habitually used
them as arms and hands for the purpose of pointing out any
object towards which he wished to direct attention; the rest
of his features were equally striking in their way, and were all

and all his own. He wore a fancy dress, partly resembling the costume of Napoleon, and partly that of a widow woman. I could not have named anybody more decidedly differing in appearance from the rest of the human race.

"Whom do you name?"—"I name John Keate."— "Now what do you see?" said the Wizard to the boy.—"I see," answered the boy, "I see a fair girl with golden hair, blue eyes, pallid face, rosy lips." *There* was a shot! I shouted out my laughter with profane exultation, and the Wizard, perceiving the grossness of his failure, declared that the boy must have known sin (for none but the innocent can see truth), and accordingly kicked him down stairs.

One or two other boys were tried, but none could "see truth."

Notwithstanding the failure of these experiments, I wished to see what sort of mummery my Magician would practise if I called upon him to show me some performances of a higher order than those already attempted. I therefore made a treaty with him, in virtue of which he was to descend with me into the tombs near the Pyramids, and there evoke the Devil. The negotiation lasted some time, for Dthemetri, as in duty bound, tried to beat down the Wizard as much as he could, and the Wizard on his part manfully stuck up for his price, declaring that to raise the Devil was really no joke, and insinuating that to do so was an awesome crime. I let Dthemetri have his way in the negotiation, but I felt in reality very indifferent about the sum to be paid, and for this reason, namely, that the payment (except a very small present which I might make, or not, as I chose) was to be *contingent on success.* At length the bargain was finished, and it was arranged that, after a few days to be allowed for preparation, the Wizard should raise the Devil for two pounds ten, play or pay—no Devil, no piastres.

The Wizard failed to keep his appointment. I sent to know why the deuce he had not come to raise the Devil. The truth was that my Mahomet had gone to the mountain. The Plague had seized him, and he died.

Although the Plague was now spreading quick and terrible havoc around him, I did not see very plainly any corresponding change in the looks of the streets until the seventh day after my arrival: I then first observed that the city was *silenced*. There were no outward signs of despair nor of violent terror, but many of the voices that had swelled the busy hum of men were already hushed in death, and the survivors, so used to scream and screech in their earnestness whenever they bought or sold, now showed an unwonted indifference about the affairs of this world: it was less worth while for men to haggle and haggle, and crack the sky with noisy bargains, when the Great Commander was there, who could "pay all their debts with the roll of his drum."

At this time I was informed that of 25,000 people at Alexandria, 12,000 had died already; the Destroyer had come rather later to Cairo, but there was nothing of weariness in his strides. The deaths came faster than ever they befell in the Plague of London; but the calmness of Orientals under such visitations, and their habit of using biers for interment instead of burying coffins along with the bodies, rendered it practicable to dispose of the dead in the usual way, without shocking the people by any unaccustomed spectacle of horror. There was no tumbling of bodies into carts, as in the Plague of Florence, and the Plague of London; every man, according to his station, was properly buried, and that in the accustomed way, except that he went to his grave at a pace more than usually rapid.

The funerals pouring through the streets were not the only public evidence of deaths. In Cairo this custom prevails:——at the instant of a man's death (if his property is sufficient to justify the expense) professional howlers are employed. I believe that these persons are brought near to the dying man, when his end appears to be approaching, and the moment that life is gone, they lift up their voices, and send forth a loud wail from the chamber of Death. Thus I knew when my near neighbours died: sometimes the howls were near; sometimes more distant. Once I was awakened in the night by the wail of death in the next house, and another time by a like howl from the house opposite; and there were two or three minutes, I recollect, during which the howl seemed to be actually *running* along the street.

I happened to be rather teazed at this time by a sore throat, and I thought it would be well to get it cured, if I could, before I again started on my travels. I therefore inquired for a Frank doctor, and was informed that the only one then at Cairo was a Bolognese Refugee, a very young practitioner, and so poor that he had not been able to take flight, as the other medical men had done. At such a time as this it was out of the question to *send* for an European physician; a person thus summoned would be sure to suppose that the patient was ill of the Plague, and would decline to come. I therefore rode to the young Doctor's residence, ascended a flight or two of stairs, and knocked at his door. No one came immediately, but after some little delay the Medico himself opened the door and admitted me. I, of course, made him understand that I had come to consult him, but before entering upon my throat grievance, I accepted a chair, and exchanged a sentence or two of common-place conversation. Now, the natural common-place of the city at this season was of a gloomy sort—"Come va la peste?" (how goes the plague?), and this was precisely the question I put. A deep sigh, and the words "Sette cento per giorno, Signor" (seven hundred a day), pronounced in a tone of the deepest sadness and dejection, were the answer I received. The day was not oppressively hot, yet I saw that the Doctor was transpiring profusely, and even the outside surface of the thick shawl dressing-gown in which he had wrapped himself appeared to be moist. He was a handsome, pleasant-looking young fellow, but the deep melancholy of his tone did not tempt me to prolong the conversation, and without farther delay, I requested that my throat might be looked at. The Medico held my chin in the usual way, and examined my throat; he then wrote me a prescription, and almost immediately afterwards I bid him farewell; but as he conducted me towards the door, I observed an expression of strange and unhappy watchfulness in his rolling eyes. It was not the next day, but the next day but one, if I rightly remember, that I sent to request another interview with my Doctor. In due time Dthemetri, my messenger, returned, looking sadly aghast. He had "met the Medico," for so he phrased it, "coming out from his house—in a bier!"

It was, of course, plain that when the poor Bolognese stood looking down my throat and almost mingling his breath with mine, he was already stricken of the Plague. I suppose that his violent sweat must have been owing to some medicine administered by himself in the faint hope of a cure. The peculiar rolling of his eyes which I had remarked is, I believe, to experienced observers a pretty sure test of the Plague. A Russian acquaintance of mine, speaking from the information of men who had made the Turkish campaigns of 1828 and 1829, told me that by this sign the officers of Sabalkansky's force were able to make out the plague-stricken soldiers with a good deal of certainty.

It so happened that most of the people with whom I had anything to do, during my stay in Cairo, were seized with Plague; and all these died. Since I had been for a long time *en route* before I reached Egypt, and was about to start again for another long journey over the Desert, there were of course many little matters touching my wardrobe and my travelling equipments which required to be attended to whilst I remained in the city. It happened so many times that Dthemetri's orders in respect to these matters were frustrated by the deaths of the tradespeople and others whom he employed, that at last I became quite accustomed to the peculiar manner of the man when he prepared to announce a new death to me. The poor fellow naturally supposed that I should feel some uneasiness at hearing of the "accidents" continually happening to persons employed by me, and he therefore communicated their deaths as though they were the deaths of friends; he would cast down his eyes, and look like a man abashed, and then gently, and with a mournful gesture, allow the words "Morto, Signor," to come through his lips. I don't know how many of such instances occurred, but they were several, and besides these (as I told you before), my banker, my doctor, my landlord, and my magician, all died of the Plague. A lad who acted as a helper in the house I occupied lost a brother and a sister within a few hours. Out of my two established donkey-boys one died. I did not hear of any instances in which a plague-stricken patient had recovered.

Going out one morning, I met unexpectedly the scorching breath of the Khamseen wind, and fearing that I should faint under the infliction, I returned to my rooms. Reflecting, however, that I might have to encounter this wind in the desert, where there would be no possibility of avoiding it, I thought it would be better to brave it once more in the city, and to try whether I could really bear it or not. I, therefore, mounted my ass, and rode to old Cairo and along the gardens by the banks of the Nile. The wind was hot to the touch as though it came from a furnace; it blew strongly, but yet with such perfect steadiness, that the trees bending under its force remained fixed in the same curves without perceptibly waving; the whole sky was obscured by a veil of yellowish gray that shut out the face of the sun. The streets were utterly silent, being indeed almost entirely deserted, and not without cause, for the scorching blast, whilst it fevers the blood, closes up the pores of the skin, and is terribly distressing therefore to every animal that encounters it. I returned to my rooms dreadfully ill. My head ached with a burning pain, and my pulse bounded quick and fitfully, but perhaps (as in the instance of the poor Levantine whose death I was mentioning) the fear and excitement I felt in trying my own wrist may have made my blood flutter the faster.

It is a thoroughly well believed theory that, during
the continuance of the Plague, you can't be ill of any other
febrile malady; an unpleasant privilege that! for ill I was, and
ill of fever; and I anxiously wished that the ailment might
turn out to be anything rather than Plague. I had some right
to surmise that my illness might have been merely the effect
of the hot wind; and this notion was encouraged by the elas-
ticity of my spirits, and by a strong forefeeling that much of
my destined life in this world was yet to come, and yet to be
fulfilled. That was my instinctive belief; but when I carefully
weighed the probabilities on the one side, and on the other, I
could not help seeing that the strength of argument was all
against me. There was a strong antecedent likelihood in
favour of my being struck by the same blow as the rest of the
people who had been dying around me. Besides, it occurred
to me that, after all, the universal opinion of the Europeans
upon a medical question, such as that of contagion, might
probably be correct; and *if it were,* I was so thoroughly "compromised," especially by the touch and breath of the dying
Medico, that I had no right to expect any other fate than

that which now seemed to have overtaken me. Balancing then as well as I could all the considerations suggested by hope and fear, I slowly and reluctantly came to the conclusion that, according to all merely reasonable probability, the Plague had come upon me.

You might suppose that this conviction would have induced me to write a few farewell lines to those who were dearest, and that having done that, I should have turned my thoughts towards the world to come. Such, however, was not the case; I believe that the prospect of death often brings with it strong anxieties about matters of comparatively trivial import, and certainly with me the whole energy of the mind was directed towards the one petty object of concealing my illness until the latest possible moment—until the delirious stage. I did not believe that either Mysseri, or Dthemetri, who had served me so faithfully in all trials, would have deserted me (as most Europeans are wont to do) when they knew that I was stricken by Plague; but I shrank from the idea of putting them to this test, and I dreaded the consternation which the knowledge of my illness would be sure to occasion.

I was very ill indeed at the moment when my dinner was served, and my soul sickened at the sight of the food, but I had luckily the habit of dispensing with the attendance of servants during my meal, and as soon as I was left alone, I made a melancholy calculation of the quantity of food I should have eaten if I had been in my usual health, and filled my plates accordingly, and gave myself salt, and so on, as though I were going to dine; I then transferred the viands to a piece of the omnipresent *Times* newspaper, and hid them away in a cupboard, for it was not yet night, and I dared not to throw the food into the street until darkness came. I did not at all relish this process of fictitious dining, but at length the cloth was removed, and I gladly reclined on my divan (I would not lie down), with the *Arabian Nights* in my hand.

I had a feeling that tea would be a capital thing for me, but I would not order it until the usual hour. When at last the time came, I drank deep draughts from the fragrant cup. The effect was almost instantaneous. A plenteous sweat burst through my skin, and watered my clothes through and through. I kept myself thickly covered. The hot tormenting weight which had been loading my brains was slowly heaved away. The fever was extinguished. I felt a new buoyancy of spirits, and an unusual activity of mind. I went into my bed under a load of thick covering, and when the morning came, and I asked myself how I was, I answered, "perfectly well."

I was very anxious to procure, if possible, some medical advice for Mysseri, whose illness prevented my departure. Every one of the European practising doctors, of whom there had been many, had either died or fled; it was said, however, that there was an Englishman in the medical service of the Pasha who quietly remained at his post, but that he never engaged in private practice. I determined to try if I could obtain assistance in this quarter. I did not venture at first, and at such a time as this, to ask him to visit a servant who was prostrate on the bed of sickness; but thinking that I might thus gain an opportunity of persuading him to attend Mysseri, I wrote a note mentioning my own affair of the sore throat, and asking for the benefit of his medical advice; he instantly followed back my messenger, and was at once shown up into my room. I entreated him to stand off, telling him fairly how deeply I was "compromised," and especially by my contact with a person actually ill, and since dead of Plague. The generous fellow, with a good-humoured laugh at the terrors of the contagionists, marched straight up to me, and forcibly seized my hand, and shook it with manly violence. I felt grateful indeed, and swelled with fresh pride of race, because that my countryman could carry himself so nobly. He soon cured Mysseri, as well as me, and all this he did from no other motives than the pleasure of doing a kindness, and the delight of braving a danger.

At length the great difficulty I had had in procuring beasts for my departure was overcome, and now, too, I was to have the new excitement of travelling on dromedaries. With two of these beasts, and three camels, I gladly wound my way from out of the pest-stricken city. As I passed through the streets, I observed a grave elder, stretching forth his arms, and lifting up his voice in a speech which seemed to have some reference to me. Requiring an interpretation, I found that the man had said, "The Pasha seeks camels, and he finds them not—the Englishman says 'let camels be brought,' and behold—there they are."

I no sooner breathed the free, wholesome air of the desert, than I felt that a great burthen which I had been scarcely conscious of bearing was lifted away from my mind. For nearly three weeks I had lived under peril of death; the peril ceased, and not till then did I know how much alarm and anxiety I had really been suffering.

Alifa Rifaat

MANSOURA

SHEIKH ZEIDAN PROPPED his scrawny backside against the pile of sand taken from the trench dug along the length of the street branching off from the central square of one of Cairo's suburbs. Pulling up the ends of his trousers, on top of which he wore a short calico shirt, from his thin legs that were like the branches of a tree from which the bark has been stripped, he engrossed himself in wrapping round them torn pieces of sacking; these he cov-

---

Alifa Rifaat is unusual among Arab women writers: she did not go to college, speaks only Arabic, and seldom travels abroad. This sheltering from the Western world gives readers an enlightening glimpse into Cairo's male-dominated society. This story is from her 1983 collection, Distant View of a Minaret.

ered over with two nylon bags, binding them all together with bits of string so as to protect himself from the putrid flow from the sewers. The vast iron pipes that he and his fellow workers were to fix in the trench were stacked on both sides of the street.

Jumping into the trench, he gave the signal to the others to start work. They jumped in behind him and spread out through the trench as they awaited the giant yellow bulldozer that was advancing towards them, a pipe suspended on high in its iron grasp that hung down from thick, metal ropes. Slowly it began its descent till it was received by several arms, which guided it to the required place. At this Sheikh Zeidan's voice was raised in a chant:

"O Mansoura, O Allah . . . O Mansoura, O Allah . . . O Mansoura, O Allah."

Animated, envigorated, the men raised their voices as they intoned the chant in a monotonous rhythm. Even the bulldozer's movements, as it went back and forth, became more energetic, as though it were the leading camel in a caravan moved by the chanting of the camel-driver. It went on bringing one pipe after another to the men in the trench and they would carefully fit the ends together so that the new sewer might come into being. Thus they continued till the sun was extinguished and the sky rusted and work came to a stop; then red warning lamps were hung on the wooden signboards that bore the name of the company entrusted with this work.

When the sky's slate split open to reveal shining stars and the *muezzin* gave the call to evening prayers, the men came out from the tent they'd set up amidst the flowerbeds and lined up behind Sheikh Zeidan. After performing their prayers, they spread out on the damp grass, giving pride of place to their Sheikh. One of the workmen rose and gathered up some broken pieces of scaffolding, making a heap of them in the middle of where they were sitting, and set them ablaze and buried the teapot amidst the glowing embers. Soon it was boiling and sending out its fragrance, while the *narghile* was carefully prepared and passed silently from mouth to mouth, each man rubbing his fingers over the mouthpiece before giving it to his neighbour; the puffs were followed by long, noisy gulps from the tin cups filled with dark, generously sugared tea. They sat in a silent circle like men performing some heathen rite. A soft clearing of the throats announced a readiness for the evening's conversation, and they waited for the customary question that was asked whenever a new workman joined them.

Dahshan, who had joined them only that morning, looked round with wondering eyes at the others, then asked abruptly:

"Who's this Mansoura, Sheikh Zeidan, whose name we invoke?"

Sheikh Zeidan gave a smile, and the men exchanged knowing glances as they waited for the Sheikh to begin telling his story as always happened on such occasions. The Sheikh, however, said:

"How extraordinary, fellows! Is there anyone who doesn't know of her great powers?"

Dahshan burst out into a shrill laugh as though excusing himself for his ignorance and said:

"Your pardon, kind people—the fact of the matter is that I'm from a village a long way from where you're from and we don't know about her."

The men laughed and the Sheikh's eyes gazed distractedly at the blazing fire.

"Good Lord—Mansoura! Is there anyone who hasn't heard of you? Let's say the Fatiha on her soul and a prayer for the Prophet."

Hands and voices were raised in supplication for mercy for that person who, whenever they fitted a pipe and asked help in her name, seemed to lighten the load for them, as though hidden wings were bearing the pipe along in their stead.

Suddenly the lights of the square came on, dispersing the darkness around them. Sheikh Zeidan clapped his hands together, saying:

"O Light of the Prophet! You see—at the mention of her the light burst forth. There wasn't a prettier girl than her. The way she had of walking brought about an earthquake in men's bodies. Their hearts would tremble as her body, lush as green lettuce, swayed to right and left carrying the earthenware jar of water. She would do the round of the houses, filling up the storage jars of the ladies who were the wives of the leading men of the village. Yes, her clothes might have been shabby but her eyes were glowing lamps. She was a bold one, never lowering her eyes like other girls when facing men. She would stare right at God's creatures as if embracing the whole world with eyes of tenderness. Everyone was in love with her but she had eyes for no one but Sayyid Abu Ghaneema, the one who owned the date palms on the borders of the village towards the mountain. Tall and broad he was like a piece of rock torn out of the mountain side; his heart was like steel and he feared neither djinn nor wolf. But when of an afternoon he would be dangling hook and line from the canal bank and he would meet her, his ruddy face would turn pale and he would lower his head. Giving that laugh of hers, she would stride off proudly. One day the wife was joking with her and the girl told her about herself and that night the wife related the story to me. In the morning I called for him and said:

"'Sayyid my son, strive for what is legal.'

"'The moon's too high up in the sky,' he said to me, 'and what's going to make it hang on the wall?'

"'You helpless boy,' I said to him, 'there's a proverb that says: "Better a man's shade than a wall's shade." Though your pocket is empty mine can look after all her demands.'

"The fellow was delighted and went off with hope in his heart, and when the wife asked Mansoura about her condition she said:

"'Auntie, I'm at the man's disposal. Sayyid's the best of men and so strong he'd tear down a mountain.'

"And so trilling cries of joy rang out and a wedding party was held and the lucky man's hut became filled with lawful plenty, for people's hearts are filled with faith and generosity. The two of them bathed in the honey of happiness after the dark night of misery."

Dahshan scratched his neck and shoved his skullcap over his forehead.

"It's true, man," he said—"it's all a matter of luck."

"But the lifespan of happiness is short, my son," said the Sheikh, "—as short as the life of a flower. The Devil went after them till he sowed mischief between them."

The Sheikh fell silent and took several sips of tea. Meanwhile Dahshan had moved across towards the Sheikh and settled himself beside him on the grass.

"For the sake of the Prophet," he said, "tell us the rest of the story of Mansoura, Uncle."

The Sheikh straightened himself and sat back on his heels. He rapped his hands against his knees.

"Why turn over what's buried and done with, my son?" he said. "I don't like talking about the honour of women."

"Man, tell us—does anything stay hidden?"

Said the Sheikh:

"When the watchman Hindawi was appointed in charge of the canal lock for the night shift, he went to Sayyid in his hut among the date palms by the mountain and said to him:

"'Date palms don't give much and you've got to be on your toes to earn a living. Mansoura's a nice girl and she deserves the best. With a bit of the sweat of your brow you could spare her doing the rounds from house to house with the water jar, her torn *galabia* all wet when the cold is at its worst. The season for the dates to ripen is still far off, so come and guard the beans I've planted in my field and I'll give you a quarter of the crop.'

"Sayyid was delighted and would spend the night on Hindawi's land, tilling it in the early hours and sleeping like the dead and leaving Mansoura on her own by night in the hut—and the nights of winter know no end. He'd go off from here with his hoe and Hindawi would come knocking at the door from there, bringing with him sweets and things that dazzle a woman's eyes. The girl would open the door to him and she'd make him tea."

"Ah, the vile, cunning fellow! And did he get the better of her, Sheikh Zeidan?"

"The Lord has ordered us to be discreet about such matters, my son. Allah alone knows whether she gave

in to him—women aren't to be trusted—or whether perhaps he took her by force and the poor girl kept quiet
about it, for such as her are weak and vulnerable. Whatever
it was, he used to stay on and wouldn't go on his way till
dawn, before Sayyid's return. Walls have ears, though, and
the story got about and lewd songs came out about her,
and the strange thing is that Sayyid would sing them and
laugh as he was hoeing Hindawi's land with the sweat of
his brow and watching over it, without knowing that the
words were talking of his own honour.

"After Sayyid had brought in the crop of beans
and had taken his share and stored it away in his hut,
Mansoura got him to swear he'd not leave her on her own
again, so he went off to Hindawi and said to him:

"'I've had enough, man—Mansoura's frightened of
the mountain wolves and wants me to stay by her.'

"Hindawi ground his teeth in rage and kept silent.
The fire of love had taken flame in his heart, and
Mansoura had become for him like a drug. He comforted
himself with the thought of the proverb that says 'Hunger's

an infidel,' and that tomorrow Sayyid would be back like a dog. Every time, though, Sayyid thought about it Mansoura would implore him not to leave her alone."

"And then what happened, Sheikh Zeidan?" said one of the men, feeding the fire with more wood, as he saw the Sheikh seemingly reluctant to continue.

"When I returned at the end of the summer," Sheikh Zeidan went on, "Mansoura had completely disappeared. They said that Sayyid was like someone who's lost his reason. He searched everywhere for her—in the fields, up in the mountains, everywhere. Everyone asked about her but no one knew where she'd gone. Some said the mountain wolves had got her, others that Sayyid had learnt what had happened and had killed her.

"Then one day, at the first light of dawn, Hindawi was standing guard when he spotted something all swollen and bloated being held back by the lock gates, something blue like a carcase of some animal thrown into the canal, being tossed about to right and left by the waves. When he looked carefully at the raised, swollen arm in which were buried rusty bangles, he knew it was Mansoura. When they brought in the body they saw that Sayyid couldn't bring himself to look at her. Instead he kept looking at Hindawi and saying nothing. At last, when they accused him of murdering her, he confessed. 'Only blood,' he said, 'washes dishonour clean.' So they put him in irons and the judge gave him three years."

Dahshan wiped the sweat from his neck and exclaimed:

"Poor fellow! By Allah, if I'd been the judge I'd have let him off. After all, what choice did he have? Only blood washes dishonour clean."

"My son," said the Sheikh, "Sayyid didn't kill her or do anything of the sort. Pride made him confess so that later he could take his revenge on the real murderer."

"Hindawi?" suggested Dahshan.

"Who else?" said the Sheikh. "No sooner had they taken Sayyid away to prison than Hindawi broke down completely. He would wander round the village calling out her name and crying like a small child that's lost its mother.

Then one night he came to me and said he couldn't go on living in the village, that Mansoura's image, with her swollen arm and the rusty bangles, was always in front of him. He then told me the real story of what had happened to Mansoura. It seems that when Sayyid gave up working for Hindawi and was with Mansoura all the time, Hindawi was eaten up with love and jealousy. He just couldn't live without her. Then one day he came across her when she was alone, filling her water jar from the canal. He asked her to find a way of being with him again, of leaving Sayyid if necessary and marrying him. She told him that what had been between them was past and done with, that she belonged to Sayyid. Blinded by desire and jealousy, he attacked her, hoping to have his way with her and to bring her back to him. It seems she slipped in the mud and fell into the canal and in a matter of seconds she'd been swallowed up by the waves and it wasn't till days later that Hindawi found her body way down by the lock. 'How could I kill Mansoura?' Hindawi had said to me in a voice choked with tears. 'How could I kill someone who was dearer to me than life?'

Anyway, Hindawi was frightened that when he came out of prison Sayyid would take his revenge of him. He therefore asked me to take him to work with me in Cairo."

Dahshan looked round at the faces of the men in alarm.

"Don't worry, my boy," Sheikh Zeidan assured him. "Hindawi's no longer in this world—it was Mansoura who took her revenge of him."

"How can the dead take revenge?" muttered Dahshan.

"I told you Mansoura had special powers," Sheikh Zeidan answered him. "It happened like this: I brought Hindawi and he joined up with us. Then one day—may you not see its like, my son—we were working just as we were doing today—the Lord of the Kaaba and these men are my witness—and Hindawi and I were in the trench and the bulldozer came up with another length of pipe. I saw Hindawi's eyes as he looked up at it, his hands held out to take hold of it. There was terror in his eyes as if he'd seen a ghost and the next moment, just as if a secret hand had loosened the cables round it, the pipe fell full on Hindawi. We managed to shift the pipe from on top of him but there was no hope. Just before he died he looked up at the bulldozer. Perhaps for him the arm of the bulldozer had become the swollen arm of Mansoura with the rusted bangles. Anyway, the only words he uttered before he died were: 'Mansoura, you cruel one.'"

Sheikh Zeidan turned to Dahshan. "So you see, my boy, why it is that we always call upon Mansoura to make the work easier for us. Mansoura, my son, has special powers."

Sheikh Zeidan stared out silently at the bulldozer crouched in the semi-darkness like some beast of burden taking its nightly rest. Then he yawned and stretched and rose to his feet.

"It's an early start tomorrow, men, and we'd better get some sleep."

He walked off into the darkness and, raising his *galabia*, made water against the bole of a casuarina tree, then washed at the tap and entered the tent.

William Burroughs

THE WESTERN LANDS

JOE IS ALERT, scanning the alley in front of him. Back in the front lines, back in Egypt. But this is a different time and place. He is breathing one-God poison here. The Muslim Arabs have taken over. The Pharaohs are dead, all their Gods crumbling to dust. Only the pyramids and temples and statues remain. . . .

This is Cairo, and he belongs to the forbidden

---

*William Burroughs's biggest books—*Junkie *and* Naked Lunch*—
are freewheeling trips into the gruesome world of drug addiction.
Burroughs, who boasts surviving a fifteen-year habit, continues to
pump out surreal, disjointed novels on the horrors of technology, sex,
and religion, including his 1987 novel,* The Western Lands.

Ismailian sect. A traveling merchant with his two body-
guards. Keeping the guide in sight, through labyrinthine
alleys and bazaars and markets, the sour stench of poverty
and a snarling, doglike hate. He is carrying a short sword, a
short ebony club and a poisoned dagger. A very important
and, I may add, dangerous assignment.

The Far Assembly was simply a small teahouse
with benches along the walls, in an isolated section of the
market. Since all the seats were full, a stranger would pass
on by. Now, as they approach, three men get up and pay
and walk out. That is their signal to come in and sit down.

This was his first meeting with Hassan i Sabbah,
who was sitting directly opposite, six feet away. He wrote
in his diary:

I had an immediate impression of austerity and
dedication, but it was a kind of dedication I had never seen
before. There was nothing of the ordinary priest-fanatic
here at all. A priest is a representative and, by the nature of
his function, a conveyor of lies. Hassan i Sabbah is the
Imam. It cannot be falsified. You notice his eyes, of a very

pale blue, washing into white. His mind is clear and devious as underground water. You are not sure where it will emerge, but when it does, you realize it could only have been just there.

Questions raised: How did the Egyptian Gods and Demons set up and activate an elaborate bureaucracy governing and controlling immortality and assigning it, on arbitrary grounds, to a chosen few? The fact that few could qualify is evidence that there was something to qualify for.

Limited and precarious immortality actually existed. For this reason no one challenged the system. They wanted to become Gods themselves, under existing conditions. In other words, they prostrated themselves before the Pharaoh and the Gods that he represented and partook of. . . .

Then come the one-God religions: Judaism, Christianity, Islam, promising immortality to everyone simply for obeying a few simple rules. Just pray, and you can't go astray. Pray and believe—believe an obvious lie, and pray to a shameless swindler.

Immortality is purpose and function. Obviously,

few can qualify. And does this Christian God stand with his worshippers? He does not. Like a cowardly officer, he keeps himself well out of the war zone, bathed in the sniveling prayers of his groveling, shit-eating worshippers—his dogs.

Beryl Markham

WEST WITH THE NIGHT

ABDULLAH ALI WAS in charge of the customs office at Alamza, the Cairo airport. He was also in charge of a small department in the Realm of Things to Come; he told fortunes, and told them well. He loved aviators with a paternal love and, in his way, he gave them guidance that put to shame even their compasses. He was a tall, spare

---

In 1936, British aviatrix Beryl Markham became the first person to fly solo westward across the Atlantic. Her acclaimed 1942 autobiography, West with the Night, *describes this and other flights through uncharted Africa. The book was reissued in 1983 after a letter by Ernest Hemingway was found, in which he admitted: "...I was completely ashamed of myself as a writer...she can write rings around all of us...."*

column of a man, dark as a mummy and almost as inscrutable. He fumbled through our papers, glanced at our luggage, and affixed all the necessary stamps. Then he led us outside the customs shed, where the official glint faded from his eyes and in its place came the esoteric glow that illumines the eyes of all true seers. He kneeled in the yellow sand of the huge aerodrome and began to make marks upon it with a polished stick. "Before she leaves," he said, "the lady must have her fortune."

Blix sighed and looked wistfully toward the city. "I'm dying of thirst—and he tells fortunes!"

"Shh! That's blasphemy."

"I see a journey," said Abdullah Ali.

"They always do," said Blix.

"The lady will fly over a great water to a strange country."

"That's an easy prediction," mumbled Blix, "with the Mediterranean just ahead."

"And she will fly alone," said Abdullah Ali.

Blix turned to me. "If I am to be abandoned,

Beryl, couldn't you make it a little closer to a bar?"

Abdullah Ali heard nothing of this irreverent comment. He went on making circles and triangles with his wizard's wand and unravelling my future as if it were already my past. His red fez bobbed up and down, his slender hands moved against the sand like foraging sparrows against snow. He was not really with us nor with the fortune either; he was back there under the shadow of the half-built Sphinx, making marks in the selfsame sand.

When we left him, the polished stick had disappeared and a pencil had taken its place. Abdullah Ali too had disappeared—or was at least transformed. That thin Egyptian with the grey suit and red fez, stooping as he walked through the door of the shed, was only a customs man.

"Do you believe him?" said Blix.

A taxicab had scurried across the airport to take us to Shepheard's Hotel. I got into the car and relaxed against the leather seat.

Who believes in fortune-tellers? Very young girls, I

thought, and very old women. I was neither of these.

"I believe it all," I said. "Why not?"

IN NINETEEN-THIRTY-SIX you could not fly over any Italian territory without permission from the Italian Government. It is true that you have to clear customs at each international border in any case, but the Italian idea was different.

The Italian idea was based upon the wistful suspicion that no foreigner (certainly no Englishman) could fly over Libya, for instance, and successfully resist the temptation to take candid camera shots of the newly contrived Fascist forts. The Italians, under Mussolini, would have been hurt indeed to know that a pilot existed (and many of them did) who had less curiosity about the Fascist forts than about the exact location of a bar of soap and a tub of hot water. The official reasoning seemed to run about like this: "An aviator who shows an interest in our fortresses is guilty of espionage, and one who does not is guilty of disrespect." I think the latter crime was, of the two, the more repugnant to the legionnaires of the flowing tunic and the gleaming button.

The symbols of war—impressive desert forts, shiny planes, beetle-browed warships—all inspire the sons of Rome, if not to gallantry, then at least to histrionics, which, in the Italian mind, are synonymous anyway. I sometimes think it must be extremely difficult for the Italian people to remain patient in the face of their armies' unwavering record of defeat (they looked so resplendent on parade). But there is little complaint.

The answer must be that the country of Caruso has lived a symbolic life for so long that the token has become indistinguishable from the fact or the deed. If an aria can suffice for a fighting heart, a riband draped on any chest can suffice for a general—and the theory of victory, for victory itself.

The one highly placed Italian I knew, and for whom I had respect—as did everybody else who knew him—was the late General Balbo. Balbo was a gentleman among Fascists, and, as such, his death was an act of Fate doubtless designed in the interests of congruity.

He was Governor of Tripolitania at the time Blix and I flew to England, but he had gone into the Southern Desert on routine inspection and so could not intercede, as he had twice done for me, in the matter of speeding our exit from Egypt to Libya.

However futile the Italian military, there is real striking power behind the rubber stamps of petty Italian officials—or there was. They kept Blix and me at Cairo, day after day, withholding our permits to cross the border into Libya. They had no reason, or gave none, and their maddening refusal to do anything whatever except to sit (I think literally) upon our passports, brought the profound observation from Blix that "there is no hell like uncertainty, and no greater menace to society than an Italian with three liras worth of authority."

It brought Blix to more than that. It exposed him to an incident that might have shattered the nerves of a less steady man.

Blix left Shepheard's Hotel each night well after

dinner and disappeared into the honeycombs of Cairo. He is a gregarious individual who loves his fellows and hates to be alone. It is one of the minor tragedies of his life that, no matter in what gay companionship the night begins, not many hours pass before he is alone again—at least in spirit. His friends may still be at his side around a table still graced by an open bottle—but they are mute and recumbent; they no longer finger their glasses, they no longer mutter about the vicissitudes of life, nor sing the joys of living it. They are silent, limp, or lachrymose, and in their midst sits Blix the Unsinkable—a monument of miserable sobriety, bleak as a lonely rock jutting from a lonely sea. Blix leaves them at last (after paying the bill) and seeks comfort in the noises of the night.

One night in Cairo Blix came across an old friend and a gentleman of doughty stock. He was the younger brother of Captain John Alcock (who, with Lieutenant Arthur Brown, made the first successful Atlantic flight), and moreover he was a crack pilot for Imperial Airways. Alcock the younger, who has rarely if ever been put hors de combat by anything that can be poured from a decanter, was the realization of one of Blix's most fervent hopes—a man to whom the undermost side of a table was an unexplored region.

At some bar—I cannot remember which, any more than Blix or Alcock could if they were asked—there began an historic session of comradely tippling and verbose good-fellowship which dissolved Time and reduced Space to an ante room. On the table between those good companions the whole of history was dissected and its mouldy carcass borne away in an empty ice bucket. International problems were solved in a word, and the direction of Fate foreseen through the crystal windows of two upturned goblets. It was a glorious adventure, but the only part I had in it came close on the dawn.

I was asleep in my room at Shepheard's when a fist hammered at my door. Ordinarily I should have climbed out of bed and groped for my flying clothes. Ordinarily that knock would have meant that somebody had forced-landed in a cotton field, probably in the middle of Uganda, and that they had communicated with Nairobi asking for a spare part. But this was Cairo, and that insistent fist must be the fist of Blix.

I groped for lights, got into a dressing-gown, and let fly a few whispered maledictions aimed at the head of Bacchus. But what I saw before me, when I opened the door, was no reeling Blix, nor even a swaying one. I have seldom seen a man so sober. He was grim, he was pale, he was Death warmed over. He shook like a harpstring.

He said: "Beryl, I hated to do it, but I had to wake you. The head rolled eight feet from the body."

There are various techniques for coping with people who say things like that. Possibly the most effective is to catch them just under the ear with a bronze book-end (preferably a cast of Rodin's "Thinker") and then scream—remembering always that the scream is of secondary importance to the book-end.

Shepheard's in Cairo is one of the most civilized hotels in the world. It has everything—lifts, restaurants, an enormous foyer, cocktail rooms, a famous bar and ballroom. But it has no book-ends. At least my room had no book-end. It had a green vase with an Egyptian motif, but I couldn't reach it.

"The damned fools just stood there," said Blix, "and stared at the blood."

I went back to my bed and sat on it. This was our sixth day in Cairo. Almost hourly either Blix or I had telephoned to see if our papers had been stamped for passage to Libya and each time we had got "no" for an answer. It was wearing us down, both in cash and nerves, but I had thought that the most redoubtable White Hunter in Africa would have survived it a little longer. And yet, as I sat on the edge of the bed, there was Blix leaning against the wall of my room with all the vitality of a bundle of wrinkled clothes awaiting the pleasure of the hotel valet. I sighed with the sorrow of it all.

"Sit down, Blix. You're a sick man."

He didn't sit. He ran a hand over his face and stared at the floor. "So I took the head," he muttered, in a low voice, "and brought it back to the body."

And so he had, poor man. He found a chair at last, and, as the daylight grew stronger, he grew stronger too, until finally I got the whole of what was in fact a tragic happening, but whose coincidence with Blix's homeward journey from his rendezvous with Alcock gave it, nonetheless, a comic touch.

Blix had not been left alone that night. Drink for drink and word for word, he had been met and matched according to the rules of his own making. At about four o'clock in the morning, hands were clasped and two suspiciously vertical gentlemen took leave of each other. I have Blix's word for it that he walked toward Shepheard's in a geometrically straight line—an undertaking that no completely sober man would even attempt. Blix said that his head was clear, but that his thoughts were complicated. He said that he was not given to visions, but that two or three times he had humanely stepped over small, nondescript animals in his path, only to realize, on looking back, how deceptive shadows can be in a dimly lighted city street.

It was not until he was within two blocks of

Shepheard's, and doing nicely, that he saw at his feet a human head completely detached from its body.

Blix's presence of mind never left him on safari, nor did it here. He merely assumed that, being a little older than he had been, all-night revelry left him more shaky than it used to do. He squared his shoulders and was about to carry on when he saw that other people stood in a circle on the concrete walk—all of them staring at the severed head and babbling so idiotically that it came to Blix with violent suddenness that neither the people nor the head was an hallucination; a man had fallen across the tramlines in the path of an onrushing car and had been decapitated.

There were no police, there was no ambulance, there was no effort on anybody's part to do anything but gape. Blix, used to violence, was not used to indifference in the face of tragedy. He kneeled on the walk, took the head in his arms, and returned it to its body. It was the body of an Egyptian labourer, and Blix stood over it pouring Swedish imprecations on the gathered onlookers, like an outraged prophet reviling his flock. And when the authorities did arrive, he left his gruesome post, stole through the crowd, with his lips clamped tightly together, and came to Shepheard's.

All this he told me while he slumped in a chair and the morning traffic of Cairo began to hum beneath my windows.

After a while I ordered some coffee and, while we drank it, I thought that anyway there was hope for the world so long as the fundamental decency of man was strong enough to triumph over all that the demon rum could do with six hours' start—and more cooperation than any demon has a right to expect.

"Are you giving up all-night parties, Blix?"

He shook his head. "Oh, but I think that would be so very rash and so very unsociable. Walking home from them is the thing to avoid—I promise you!"

William Thackeray

TO CAIRO

THIS, AS AN account of Cairo, dear M. ——, you will probably be disposed to consider as incomplete: the fact is, I have seen nothing else as yet. I have peered into no harems. The magicians, proved to be humbugs, have been bastinadoed out of town. The dancing girls, those lovely Alme, of whom I had hoped to be able to give a glowing and elegant, though strictly moral, description, have been whipped into Upper Egypt, and as you are saying in

---

English novelist William Thackeray is best known for his satires of middle-class England, Vanity Fair *and* The Virginians. *In 1844, he embarked on a lengthy Mediterranean journey, the notes of which are collected in* Cornhill to Grand Cairo.

your mind * * Well it *isn't* a good description of Cairo;
you are perfectly right. It is England in Egypt? I like to see
her there with her pluck, enterprise, manliness, bitter ale
and Harvey sauce. Wherever they come they stay and pros-
per. From the summit of yonder pyramids forty centuries
may look down on them if they are minded; and I say,
those venerable daughters of time ought to be better
pleased by the examination, than by regarding the French
bayonets and General Bonaparte, Member of the Institute,
fifty years ago, running about with sabre and pigtail.
Wonders he did to be sure, and then ran away, leaving
Klèber, to be murdered, in the lurch—a few hundred yards
from the spot where these disquisitions are written. But
what are his wonders compared to Waghorn? Nap. massacred the Mamelukes at the pyramids: Wag. has conquered
the pyramids themselves; dragged the unwieldly structures a
month nearer England than they were, and brought the
country along with them. All the trophies and captives,
that ever were brought to Roman triumph, were not so
enormous and wonderful as this. All the heads that

Napoleon ever caused to be struck off (as George Cruikshank says) would not elevate him a monument as big. Be ours the trophies of peace! O my country! O Waghorn! *Hae tibi erunt artes.* When I go to the pyramids I will sacrifice in your name, and pour out libations of bitter ale and Harvey sauce in your honour.

One of the noblest views in the world is to be seen from the citadel, which we ascended today. You see the city stretching beneath it, with a thousand minarets and mosques,—the great river curling through the green plains, studded with innumerable villages. The pyramids are beyond, brilliantly distinct; and the lines and fortifications of the height, and the arsenal lying below. Gazing down, the guide does not fail to point out the famous Mameluke leap, by which one of the corps escaped death, at the time that his Highness the Pasha arranged the general massacre.

The venerable Patriarch's harem is close by, where he received, with much distinction, some of the members of our party. We were allowed to pass very close to the sacred precincts, and saw a comfortable white European building, approached by flights of steps, and flanked by pretty gardens. Police and law-courts were here also, as I understood; but it was not the time of Egyptian assizes. It would have been pleasant, otherwise, to see the chief Cadi in his hall of justice; and painful though instructive, to behold the immediate application of the bastinado.

The great lion of the place is a new mosque which Mehemet Ali is constructing very leisurely. It is built of alabaster of a fair white, with a delicate blushing tinge; but the ornaments are European—the noble, fantastic, beautiful Oriental art is forgotten. The old mosques of the city, of which I entered two, and looked at many, are a thousand times more beautiful. Their variety of ornament is astonishing,—the difference in the shapes of the domes, the beautiful fancies and caprices in the forms of the minarets, which violate the rules of proportion with the most happy, daring grace, must have struck every architect who has seen them. As you go through the streets, these architectural beauties keep the eye continually charmed: now it is a marble fountain, with its arabesque and carved overhanging roof, which you can look at with as much pleasure as an antique gem, so neat and brilliant is the execution of it; then, you come to the arched entrance to a mosque, which shoots up like—like what?—like the most beautiful pirouette by Taglioni, let us say. This architecture is not sublimely beautiful, perfect loveliness and calm, like that which was revealed to us at the Parthenon (and in comparison of which the Pantheon and Colosseum are vulgar and coarse, mere broad-shouldered Titans before ambrosial Jove); but these fantastic spires, and cupolas, and galleries, excite, amuse, *tickle* the imagination so to speak, and perpetually fascinate the eye. There were very few believers in the famous mosque of Sultan Hassan when we visited it, except the moslem beadle, who was on the look out for *backsheesh*, just like his brother officer in an English cathedral; and who, making us put on straw slippers, so as not to pollute the sacred pavement of the place, conducted us through it.

It is stupendously light and airy; the best specimens of Norman art that I have seen (and surely the Crusaders must have carried home the models of these heathenish temples in their eyes) do not exceed its noble grace and simplicity. The mystics make discoveries at home, that the Gothic architecture is Catholicism carved in stone (in which case, and if architectural beauty is a criterion or expression of religion, what a dismal barbarous creed must that, expressed by the Bethesda meeting-house and Independent chapels, be?); if, as they would gravely hint, because Gothic architecture is beautiful, Catholicism is therefore lovely and right,—why, Mahommedanism must have been right and lovely too once. Never did a creed possess temples more elegant; as elegant as the Cathedral at Rouen, or the Baptistery at Pisa.

But it is changed now. There was nobody at prayers; only the official beadles, and the supernumerary guides, who came for *backsheesh*. Faith has degenerated. Accordingly they can't build these mosques, or invent these perfect forms, any more. Witness the tawdry incompleteness and vulgarity of the Pasha's new temple, and the woeful failures among the very late edifices in Constantinople!

However, they still make pilgrimages to Mecca in

great force. The mosque of Hassan is hard by the green plain on which the *Hajj* encamps before its set forth annually on its pious perigrination. It was not yet its time, but I saw in the bazaars that redoubted Dervish, who is the Master of the *Hajj*—the leader of every procession, accompanying the sacred camel; and a personage almost as much respected as Mr. O'Connell in Ireland.

This fellow lives by alms (I mean the head of the *Hajj*). Winter and summer he wears no clothes but a thin and scanty white shirt. He wields a staff, and stalks along scowling and barefoot. His immense shock of black hair streams behind him, and his brown, brawny body is curled over with black hair, like a savage man. This saint has the largest harem in the town; he is said to be enormously rich by the contributions he has levied; and is so adored for his holiness by the infatuated folk, that when he returns from the *Hajj* (which he does on horseback, the chief Mollahs going out to meet him and escort him home in state along the Ezbekieh road), the people fling themselves down under the horse's feet, eager to be trampled upon and killed, and confident of Heaven if the great Hajji's horse will but kick them into it. Was it my fault if I thought of Hajji Daniel, and the believers in him.

There was no Dervish of repute on the plain when I passed; only one poor, wild fellow, who was dancing, with glaring eyes and grizzled beard, rather to the contempt of the by-standers, as I thought, who by no means put coppers into his extended bowl. On this poor devil's head there was a poorer devil still—a live cock, entirely plucked, but ornamented with some bits of ragged tape and scarlet and tinsel, the most horribly grotesque and miserable object I ever saw.

A little way from him, there was a sort of play going on—a clown and a knowing one, like Widdicombe and the clown with us,—the buffoon answering with blundering responses, which made all the audience shout with laughter; but the only joke which was translated to me would make you do anything but laugh, and shall therefore never be revealed by these lips. All their humour, my dragoman tells me, is of this questionable sort; and a young

Egyptian gentleman, son of a Pasha, whom I subsequently met at Malta, confirmed the statement, and gave a detail of the practices of private life, which was anything but edifying. The great aim of the women, he said, in the much maligned Orient, is to administer to the brutality of her lord; her merit is in knowing how to vary the beast's pleasures. He could give us no idea, he said, of the *wit* of the Egyptian women, and their skill in *double entendre*; nor, I presume, did we lose much by our ignorance. What I would urge, humbly, however, is this—Do not let us be led away by German writers and aesthetics, Semilassoisms, Hahnhahnisms, and the like. The life of the East is a life of brutes. The much-maligned Orient, I am confident, has not been maligned near enough; for the good reason that none of us can tell the amount of horrible sensuality practised there.

Beyond the jack pudding rascal and his audience, there was on the green a spot, on which was pointed out to me, a mark, as of blood. That morning the blood had spouted from the neck of an Arnaoot soldier, who had been executed for murder. The Arnaoots are the curse and terror of the citizens. Their camps are without the city; but they are always brawling, or drunken, or murdering within, in spite of the rigid law which is applied to them, and which brings one or more of the scoundrels to death almost every week.

Some of our party had seen this fellow borne by the hotel the day before, in the midst of a crowd of soldiers who had apprehended him. The man was still formidable to his score of captors; his clothes had been torn off; his limbs were bound with cords; but he was struggling frantically to get free; and my informant described the figure and appearance of the naked, bound, writhing savage, as quite a model of beauty.

Walking in the street, this fellow had just before been struck by the looks of a woman who was passing, and laid hands on her. She ran away, and he pursued her. She ran into the police barrack, which was luckily hard by; but the Arnaoot was nothing daunted, and followed into the midst of the police. One of them tried to stop him. The

Arnaoot pulled out a pistol, and shot the policeman dead. He cut down three or four more before he was secured. He knew his inevitable end must be death: that he could not seize upon the woman: that he could not hope to resist half a regiment of armed soldiers: yet his instinct of lust and murder was too strong; and so he had his head taken off quite calmly this morning, many of his comrades attending their brother's last moments. He cared not the least about dying; and knelt down and had his head off as coolly as if he were looking on at the same ceremony performed on another.

When the head was off, and the blood was spouting on the ground, a married woman, who had no children, came forward very eagerly out of the crowd, to smear herself with it,——the application of criminals' blood being considered a very favourable medicine for women afflicted with barrenness,——so she indulged in this remedy.

But one of the Arnaoots, standing near, said "What, you like blood, do you? (or words to that effect) Let's see how yours mixes with my comrade's" and thereupon, taking out a pistol, he shot the woman in the midst of the crowd and the guards who were attending the execution; was seized of course by the latter; and no doubt tomorrow morning will have his head off too. It would be a good chapter to write—the *Death of the Arnaoot*—but I shan't go. Seeing one man hanged is quite enough in the course of a life. *J'y ai été*, as the Frenchman said of hunting.

These Arnaoots are the terror of the town. They seized hold of an Englishman the other day, and were very nearly pistolling him. Last week one of them murdered a shopkeeper at Boulak, who refused to sell him a watermelon at a price which he, the soldier, fixed upon it. So, for the matter of three half-pence, he killed the shopkeeper; and had his own rascally head chopped off, universally regretted by his friends. Why, I wonder, does not his Highness the Pasha invite the Arnaoots to a *déjeuner* at the Citadel, as he did the *Mamluks*, and serve them up the same sort of breakfast? The walls are considerably heightened since Emin Bey and his horse leapt them, and it is probable that not one of them would escape.

EVERYBODY HAS BIG rolling eyes here (unless to be sure they lose one of ophthalmia). The Arab women are some of the noblest figures I have ever seen. The habit of carrying jars on the head always gives the figure grace and motion; and the dress the women wear certainly displays it to full advantage. I have brought a complete one home with me, at the service of any lady for a masqued ball. It consists of a coarse blue dress of calico, opened in front, and fastened with a horn button. Three yards of blue stuff for a veil; on the top of the veil a jar to be balanced on the head; and a little black strip of silk to fall over the nose, and leave the beautiful eyes full of liberty to roll and roam. But such a costume, not aided by any stays or any other article of dress whatever, can be worn only by a very good figure. I suspect it won't be borrowed for many balls next season.

The men, a tall handsome noble race, are treated like dogs. I shall never forget riding through the crowded bazaars, my interpreter, or *laquais de place*, ahead of me to clear the way—when he took his whip, and struck it over the shoulders of a man who could not or would not make way!

The man turned round—an old, venerable, handsome face, with awfully sad eyes, and a beard long and quite grey. He did not make the least complaint, but slunk out of the way, piteously shaking his shoulder. The sight of that indignity gave me a sickening feeling of disgust. I shouted out to the cursed lackey to hold his hand, and forbade him ever in my presence to strike old or young more; but everybody is doing it. The whip is in everybody's hands: the pasha's running footman, as he goes bustling through the bazaar; the doctor's attendant, as he soberly threads the crowd on his mare; the negro slave, who is riding by himself, the most insolent of all, strikes and slashes about without mercy, and you never hear a single complaint.

How to describe the beauty of the streets to you!—the fantastic splendour; the variety of the houses, and archways, and hanging roofs, and balconies, and porches; the delightful accidents of light and shade which chequer them; the noise, the bustle, the brilliancy of the crowd; the interminable vast bazaars with their barbaric splendour! There is a fortune to be made for painters in Cairo, and materials for a whole Academy of them. I never saw such a variety of architecture, of life, of picturesqueness, of brilliant colour, and light and shade. There is a picture in every street, and at every bazaar stall. Some of these, our celebrated water-colour painter, Mr. Lewis, has produced with admirable truth and exceeding minuteness and beauty; but there is room for a hundred to follow him; and should any artist (by some rare occurrence) read this, who has leisure, and wants to break new ground, let him take heart, and try a winter in Cairo, where there is the finest climate and the best subjects for his pencil.

A series of studies of negroes alone, would form a picture-book delightfully grotesque. Mounting my donkey today, I took a ride to the desolate, noble old buildings outside the city, known as the Tombs of the Caliphs. Every one of these edifices, with their domes, and courts, and minarets is strange and beautiful. In one of them there was an encampment of negro slaves newly arrived: some scores of them were huddled against the sunny wall; two or three of their masters lounged about the court, or lay smoking upon carpets. There was one of these fellows, a straight-nosed ebony-faced Abyssinian, with an expression of such sinister, good humour in his handsome face, as would form a perfect type of villainy. He sat leering at me, over his carpet, as I endeavoured to get a sketch of that incarnate rascality. "Give me some money," said the fellow. "I know what you are about. You will sell my picture for money when you get back to Europe; let me have some of it now!" But the very rude and humble designer was quite unequal to depict such a consummation and perfection of roguery; so flung him a cigar, which he began to smoke, grinning at the giver. I requested the interpreter to inform him, by way of assurance of my disinterestedness, that his face was a great deal too ugly to be popular in Europe, and that was the particular reason why I had selected it.

Then one of his companions got up and showed

us his black cattle. The male slaves were chiefly lads, and the women young, well formed, and abominably hideous; the dealer pulled her blanket off one of them and bade her stand up, which she did with a great deal of shuddering modesty. She was coal black, her lips were the size of sausages, her eyes large and good-humoured; the hair or wool on this young person's head was curled and greased into a thousand filthy little ringlets. She was evidently the beauty of the flock.

They are not unhappy; they look to being bought, as many a spinster looks to an establishment in England; once in a family they are kindly treated and well clothed, and fatten, and are the merriest people of the whole community. These were of a much more savage sort than the slaves I had seen in the horrible market at Constantinople where I recollect the following young creature—(indeed it is a very fair likeness of her) whilst I was looking at her and forming pathetic conjectures regarding her fate—smiling very good humouredly, and bidding the interpreter ask me to buy her for twenty pounds.

From these Tombs of the Caliphs the Desert is before you. It comes up to the walls of the city, and stops at some gardens which spring up all of a sudden at its edge. You can see the first station house on the Suez Road; and so from distance point, to point, could ride thither alone without a guide.

Asinus trotted gallantly into this desert for the space of a quarter of an hour. There we were (taking care to keep our backs to the city walls), in the real actual desert: mounds upon mounds of sand, stretching away as far as the eye can see, until the dreary prospect fades away in the yellow horizon! I had formed a finer idea of it out of *Eothen*. Perhaps in a *simoom* it may look more awful. The only adventure that befell in this romantic place was that asinus' legs went deep into a hole: whereupon his rider went over his head, and bit the sand, and measured his length there; and upon this hint rose up, and rode home again. No doubt one should have gone out for a couple of days' march—as it was, the desert did not seem to me sublime, only *uncomfortable*.

Very soon after this perilous adventure the sun

likewise dipped into the sand (but not to rise therefrom so quickly as I had done); and I saw this daily phenomenon of sunset with pleasure, for I was engaged at that hour to dine with our old friend J. ——, who has established himself here in the most complete Oriental fashion.

You remember J. ——, and what a dandy he was, the faultlessness of his boots and cravats, the brilliancy of his waistcoats and kid gloves; we have seen his splendour in Regent Street, in the Tuilleries, or on the Toledo. My first object on arriving here was to find out his house, which he has taken far away from the haunts of European civilization, in the Arab quarter. It is situated in a cool, shady, narrow alley; so narrow, that it was with great difficulty— His Highness Ibrahim Pasha happening to pass at the same moment—that my little procession of two donkeys mounted by self and *valet de place*, with the two donkey-boys, our attendants, could range ourselves along the wall, and leave room for the august cavalcade. His Highness having rushed on (with an affable and good humoured salute to our imposing party), we made J. ——'s quarters; and, in the first place, entered a broad covered court or porch, where a swarthy tawny attendant, dressed in blue, with white turban, keeps a perpetual watch. Servants in the east lie about all the doors, it appears; and you clap your hands, as they do in the dear old *Arabian Nights*, to summon them.

This servant disappeared through a narrow wicket, which he closed after him; and went into the inner chambers to ask if his lord would receive us. He came back presently, and rising up from my donkey, I confided him to his attendant (lads more sharp, arch, and wicked, than these donkey-boys don't walk the *pavé* of Paris or London), and passed the mysterious outer door.

First we came into a broad open court, with a covered gallery running along one side of it. A camel was reclining on the grass there; near him was a gazelle to glad J. —— with his dark blue eye; and a numerous brood of hens and chickens, who furnish his liberal table. On the opposite side of the covered gallery rose up the walls of his long, queer, many-windowed, many-galleried house. There were wooden lattices to those arched windows, through the diamonds of one of which I saw two of the most beautiful, enormous, ogling, black eyes in the world, looking down upon the interesting stranger. Pigeons were flapping, and hopping, and fluttering, and cooing about. Happy pigeons you are, no doubt, fed with crumbs from the henna-tipped fingers of Zuleikah! All this court, cheerful in the sunshine, cheerful with the astonishing brilliancy of the eyes peering out from the lattice bars, was as mouldy, ancient, and ruinous, as any gentleman's house in Ireland, let us say. The paint was peeling off the rickety, old, carved, galleries; the arabesques over the windows were chipped and worn;—the ancientness of the place rendered it doubly picturesque. I have detained you a long time in the outer court. Why the deuce was Zuleikah there, with the beautiful black eyes!

Hence we passed into a large apartment, where there was a fountain; and another domestic made his appearance, taking me in charge, and relieving the tawny porter of the gate. This fellow was clad in blue too, with a red sash and a grey beard. He conducted me into a great hall, where there was a great, large Saracen oriel window.

He seated me on a divan; and stalking off, for a moment, returned with a long pipe and brass chafing dish: he blew the coal for the pipe, which he motioned me to smoke, and left me there with a respectful bow. This delay, this mystery of servants, that outer court with the camels, gazelles, and other beautiful-eyed things, affected me prodigiously all the time he was staying away; and while I was examining the strange apartment and its contents, my respect and awe for the owner increased vastly.

As you will be glad to know how an Oriental nobleman (such as J. —— undoubtedly is) is lodged and garnished, let me describe the contents of this hall of audience. It is about forty feet long, and eighteen or twenty high. All the ceiling is carved, gilt, painted and embroidered with arabesques, and choice sentences of Eastern writing. Some Mameluke Aga, or Bey, whom Mehemet Ali invited to breakfast and massacred, was the proprietor of this mansion once; it has grown dingier, but, perhaps, handsomer, since his time. Opposite the divan is a great bay-window, with a divan likewise round the niche. It looks out upon a garden about the size of Fountain Court, Temple; surrounded by the tall houses of the quarter. The garden is full of green. A great palm tree springs up in the midst, with plentiful shrubberies, and a talking fountain. The room besides the divan is furnished with one deal table, value, five shillings; four wooden chairs, value, six shillings; and a couple of mats and carpets. The tables and chairs are luxuries imported from Europe. The regular Oriental dinner is put upon copper trays, which are laid upon low stools. Hence J. —— Effendi's house may be said to be much more sumptuously furnished than those of the Beys and Agas his neighbours.

When these things had been examined at leisure, J. —— appeared. Could it be the exquisite of the *Europa* and the *Trois Frères?* A man—in a long yellow gown, with a long beard, somewhat tinged with grey, with his head shaved, and wearing on it first a white wadded cotton nightcap, second, a red tarboosh—made his appearance and welcomed me cordially. It was some time, as the Americans say, before I could "realise" the *semillant* J. —— of old times.

He shuffled off his outer slippers before he curled up on the divan beside me. He clapped his hands, and languidly called "Mustapha." Mustapha came with more lights, pipes, and coffee; and then we fell to talking about London, and I gave him the last news of the comrades in that dear city. As we talked, his oriental coolness and languor gave way to British cordiality; he was the most amusing companion of the ———— club once more.

He has adapted himself outwardly, however, to the oriental life. When he goes abroad he rides a grey horse with red housings, and has two servants to walk beside him. He wears a very handsome grave costume of dark blue, consisting of an embroidered jacket and gaiters, and a pair of trousers, which would make a set of dresses for an English family. His beard curls nobly over his chest, his Damascus scimitar on his thigh. His red cap gives him a venerable and Bey-like appearance. There is no gewgaw or parade about him, as in some of your dandified young agas. I should say that he is a Major General of Engineers, or a grave officer of State. We and the Turkified European, who found us at dinner, sat smoking in solemn divan.

His dinners were excellent; they were cooked by a regular Egyptian female cook. We had delicate cucumbers stuffed with forced meats; yellow smoking pilaffs, the pride of the oriental cuisine; kid and fowls *à l'Aboukir* and *à la Pyramide*; a number of little savoury plates of *légumes* of the vegetable-marrow sort; kibobs with an excellent sauce of plums and piquant herbs. We ended the repast with ruby pomegranates, pulled to pieces, deliciously cool and pleasant. For the meats, we certainly ate them with the Infidel knife and fork; but for the fruit, we put our hands into the dish and flicked them into our mouths in what cannot but be the true oriental manner. I asked for lamb and pistachio nuts, and cream tarts *au poivre*; but J. ———'s cook did not furnish us with either of those historic dishes. And for drink, we had water freshened in the porous little pots of grey clay, at whose spout every traveller in the East has sucked delighted. Also it must be confessed, we drank certain sherbets, prepared by the two great rivals, Hadji Hodson and Bass Bey—the bitterest and most delicious of draughts! O divine Hodson! a camel's load of thy beer came from Beyrout to Jerusalem while we were there. How shall I ever forget the joy inspired by one of those foaming cool flasks?

We don't know the luxury of thirst in English climes. Sedentary men in cities at least have seldom ascertained it; but when they travel, our countrymen guard against it well. The road between Cairo and Suez is *jonché* with soda-water corks. Tom Thumb and his brothers might track their way across the desert by those land marks.

Cairo is magnificently picturesque: it is fine to have palm trees in your gardens, and ride about on a camel; but, after all, I was anxious to know what were the particular excitements of Eastern life, which detained J. ———, who is a town-bred man, from his natural pleasures and occupations in London; where his family don't hear from him, where his room is still kept ready at home, and his name is on the list of his Club; and where his neglected sisters tremble to think that their Frederick is going about with a great beard and a crooked sword, dressed up like an odious Turk. In a "lark" such a costume may be very well; but home, London, a razor, your sister to make tea, a pair of moderate Christian breeches in lieu of those enormous Turkish *shulwars*, are vastly more convenient in the long run. What was it that kept him away from these decent and accustomed delights?

It couldn't be the black eyes in the balcony—upon his honour she was only the black cook, who has done the pilaff, and stuffed the cucumbers. No, it was an indulgence of laziness such as Europeans, Englishmen at least, don't know how to enjoy. Here he lives like a languid Lotus-eater—a dreamy, hazy, lazy, tobaccofied life. He was away from evening parties, he said: he needn't wear white-kid gloves, or starched neckcloths, or read a newspaper. And even this life at Cairo was too civilized for him; Englishmen passed through; old acquaintances would call: the great pleasure of pleasures was life in the desert,—under the tents, with still *more* nothing to do than in Cairo; now smoking, now cantering on Arabs, and no crowd to jostle you; solemn contemplations of the stars at night, as the camels were picketed, and the fires and the pipes were lighted.

The night scene in the city is very striking for its vastness and loneliness. Everybody has gone to rest long before ten o'clock. There are no lights in the enormous buildings; only the stars blazing above, with their astonishing brilliancy, in the blue, peaceful sky. Your guides carry a couple of little lanterns, which redouble the darkness in the solitary, echoing street. Mysterious people are curled up and sleeping in the porches. A patrol of soldiers passes, and hails you. There is a light yet in one mosque, where some devotees are at prayers all night; and you hear the queerest nasal music proceeding from those pious believers. As you pass the mad-house, there is one poor fellow still talking to the moon—no sleep for him. He howls and sings there all the night—quite cheerfully, however. He has not lost his vanity with his reason; he is a Prince in spite of the bars and the straw.

What to say about those famous edifices, which has not been better said elsewhere?—but you will not believe that we visited them, unless I bring some token from them. Here is one:—

THAT WHITE-CAPPED lad skipped up the stones with a jug of water in his hand, to refresh weary climbers; and, squatting himself down on the summit, was designed as you see. The vast, flat landscape stretches behind him; the great winding river; the purple city, with forts, and domes, and spires; the green fields, and palm groves, and speckled villages; the plains still covered with shining inundations—the landscape stretches far, far away, until it is lost and mingled in the golden horizon. It is poor work this landscape painting in print. Shelley's two sonnets are the best views that I know of the Pyramids—better than reality; for a man may lay down the book, and in quiet fancy conjure up a picture out of these magnificent words, which shan't be disturbed by any pettiness or mean realities,—such as the swarms of howling beggars, who jostle you about the actual place, and scream in your ears incessantly, and hang on your skirts, and bawl for money.

Yehia Hakki

AN EMPTY BED

IF YOU TURN out of the Imamein Square into El
Rihan Street, and take only a few steps forward, you will
come, on your left hand side, to a small shop which you
will not notice as you walk past, for it is one of a close-set
indistinguishable row of shabby shops, marching exactly in
step with the narrow, dilapidated pavement, in every one of

*Yehia Hakki has a reputation as an extremely meticulous writer, one
who produces little. This lack of mass has not affected his influence,
though: Hakki continues to have a profound effect on young Arab
writers. This story first appeared in the premier issue of the review
Al Katib in 1961. Hakki currently lives in Cairo and edits Al
Magalla, Cairo's cultural monthly.*

its twists and turns, and every one of its straight runs. This shop and its companions are enveloped in a tattered web of murkiness, woven by a spider long-since dead, and since lodged in, first by coincidence and prosperity, then by sloth and by hard times. The springs that set the puppets in motion behind the shop-fronts have grown rusty. A head hangs down upon a breast. A pair of eyelids move like cumbersome door-bolts, pulled upwards by cords and then falling heavily back into place. A hand trembles as it shunts from the task of receiving small coinage to the task of handing over a customer's purchase, and then to driving away the flies which are trying to drink their fill of the saliva that dribbles down between the lips, and the rheum at the corner of an eyelid, and the ropy fluid with the attractive glossy colour, which ouzes out of the channel of an ear.

If you raise your eyes slightly as you walk past this particular shop, and you catch sight of the signboard above it, it will dispirit you: you will avert your glance and hurry onward—even if you are someone who can walk in scarcely anything more than a decrepit shuffle. Worried, you will exclaim to yourself, "This cursed employment, squeezing itself in among shops that are carrying on the sort of decent trades that are praised in the Holy Book and praised by the Prophet, shops whose owners you wouldn't hesitate to shake hands with and sit down with to a meal. It's all wrong that this shop should be here: a pimple on a smooth cheek, a whore among chaste women, a leper in the harem of an oriental potentate—one who, as though his mere presence were not bad enough, gets drunk on fresh milk handed to him by a noble-blooded pimp."

Luckily for you, your fit of depression will be driven away by your pride in your own powers of deduction; you will think yourself the first passer-by sharp enough to have noticed that the signboard must originally have hung over another shop that was broader in its frontage, for it juts out left and right over the two neighbouring shop-fronts—a comparatively modest form of encroachment upon them on its part, for its shadow covers the whole stretch of ground below. Leaning forward slightly, and with a very pronounced list to one side, the signboard might be on the verge of tumbling down; and yet it has hung there throughout the years.

The shop to the right is a small grocery store that supplies local produce. Just inside is a dusty counter of blistered wood on which you can see some pickled aubergines; every one of them has overripe seeds spilling out of its guts, while the decomposed flesh of the vegetable is falling apart in shreds, making the mouth of a customer water if he is of the vulture or of the hyena kind.

The shop on the left belongs to a leather-worker who makes bags, a craftsman in the left-overs of the butcher's trade, for the lid on one bag is the flank of a cow, the body of the next is the belly of a goat—suitcases made for separations, bags to hasten departures; strewn over railway platforms, squeezed into luggage racks, they roam the earth like homeless souls.

A donkey-cart lumbers past, giving off a faint odour of toddy; a chicken-coop without a roof or sides, crammed with black-garbed women, every one of them brooding upon her egg—and God help her if it does not hatch out, for they are, every one, involved in a race against a thieving kite, forever voracious, ever hovering patiently to swoop down upon their chicks. The donkey that draws the cart is bony and underfed; you can tell that the driver, although he is short of wind, is an insatiably avaricious person.

You glance back at the signboard once more before it passes out of your sight, at the sprawling, ornate *thuluth*, letters of its inscription, daubed on in white paint which is full of cracks that give it a tortoise-shell pattern: UNDERTAKER FOR WHOLE OF IMAMEIN DISTRICT.

The master-undertaker's apprentice leaves the shop entrance for the inner depths, a dark cave inside which the glances of a passer-by dissolve in thin air: he returns carrying on his shoulder a brand-new coffin together with its wrapping cloth, and hangs them both up on a nail upon one flap of the shop-door. Then he sits down, and polishes his nails by rubbing them against his striped *gallabiyya*.

OPPOSITE THE SHOP there have lived for a long time a small family: the father, the mother, and their only son—for the firstborn had also been the last. The neighbours do not know much about them. They realize that the family wish to lead a retired life and believe that people who withdraw in that way want to conceal very great happiness, or else very deep grief, either of which is a mortifying stigma for any unobtrusive person to live with. Those who say that there is happiness behind the veil of privacy claim that you can sense this; in any case, they add, it is plain to your own eyes when it bursts into view on saints' days and at feasts, for on those occasions there stream down from the windows of that home a festive blaze of lights and a reverberating laughter that have no equal in the entire quarter. Those who hold that there is unhappiness behind the screen of privacy point to an event that recurs once or twice a month. There draws up at the door an old car battered in body and spirit, with the air of a pregnant woman whose child has been smothered to death in her womb: a mother who gives birth to death, where others produce new life. Out of the car steps a huge-bodied attendant, in charge of a tall thin man with a sallow face, a shifty glance, and hair in wild disorder.

He is always slyly on the look-out for the moment when he can regain his freedom, and fly off in pursuit of an enemy who has destroyed his spirit, his consciousness and his reasoning powers, and left him a flair for using language as disgusting as a piece of chewed sugar-cane which has been spat out—words that he masticates with relish as his peculiar form of self-expression. The trouble is that he does not know who that enemy is. He grips hold of the car-door, then of the front door of the house; the attendant hauls him away, and with the palms of his hands, sets the man's face looking forwards so that he shall not twist his neck, and so that passers-by might be protected from the looks which he shoots at them like bullets and the foul language which would disgrace the most disreputable brothel.

When this outcry starts up, all the windows in the house slam shut at one and the same instant, as though they did so automatically and without anyone touching them. An hour or two later, the attendant emerges, still chewing the remains of a meal, wiping his moustache with one hand, his other hand held tight by the gentle, tender clasp of a tall emaciated child with a gentle soft look, who takes his seat in the car, and gives a quiet little gasp, as though he has just come back from a long ride on a lame horse and has found his own familiar bed waiting for him.

Those who maintain that the family has a secret grief assert with a discoverer's exultation and with the triumph of a gambler who has won a bet, that this is the man of distinction whom the family has produced, a man whose great fortune alone prevents them from praying earnestly for his death, since our religious law does not allow a killer to inherit the wealth of his victim, even if he kills him out of mercy for him.

It often happens that after the car moves off, the bottle-washer comes out of the café carrying a pail brimful of slops out of the hubble-bubbles. He stands on the pavement and empties his pail in one powerful sweep, and the earth feels a delightful tingle, as the water splatters down upon its skin while the aroma of the dottle spreads out like an opiate soothing the nerves of all creatures who are passing by—men, horses, mules, and donkeys alike.

THE TRUTH IS simpler than any of the surmises which have been made. The veil of secrecy had been drawn, not to hide any happiness or grief, but for another purpose, which has never been uncovered in spite of all the ingenious guess-work, and because it is more plausible, and truer to human nature—for deception plays with illusions and not with the truth, and makes fancied things shine brightly so as to dim realities. The family have chosen the only observance which requires a screen to be drawn round it if its rites are not to be disturbed and their effects nullified. They have broken with the world of men. To them it is a hornets' nest which you must keep clear of, a landmine which does you no harm so long as you merely walk around it, but which you must never touch, a sealed wineskin with the promise of a deliciously intoxicating bouquet, which when you break it open, transforms itself, and your mind with it, into floating vapours of lightheadedness. For them, life is not a vertical progress in which the new builds itself up upon the old and from which you can view an ever-widening horizon as you climb upwards. Neither is it the circling orbit of a planet, rising, climbing to its zenith, sinking, and then setting. It is, instead, a faint horizontal line, made up of a myriad of identical dark spots, soldered together so thoroughly that you can no longer make out any colour in them. Even their food is chewed for them in advance by mincing-machines and pestles: they eat meat and vegetables all pounded into one soggy mash; what they relish is the way that every ingredient loses its distinctive flavour. Opting out of life was their way of escape from direct confrontation with the most powerful and unconditional form of a grace, to which they would otherwise have had to bow down their heads as low as the earth and never raise their foreheads. This would have been a wearisome posture, and weariness is the broadest of the gates through which faithlessness finds its way in. In their rejection of a professed blessing, they acknowledge its value more so than others; they are far more conscious of an obligation which should be owed in return.

They had disengaged themselves because of a fear of receiving, as a recompense, something in whose aridity they might drown, or in whose floodwaters they might be sucked dry. They were trying to ensure in this way that they would be free from mental distress, safe from regrets at the monstrous faithlessness of others, or from grief at the baseness which they would discover in their own personalities if they ever stood in abject fear of the lassitude which lay in wait for them, and which would pin them down in terror as a snake does a sparrow. For you may stake your life upon your always remaining a stingy cowardly creature, but you dare not venture so much as a farthing upon your remaining—always and in all circumstances—courageous and generous. Having withdrawn from others, they no longer distinguish one day from another by name: they tell the passing of the days by the way in which the shadows, cast by familiar objects, gradually circle round in an arc, by identifying the calls of migrant birds: for those who cut themselves off from the world of men draw closer to nature. As the days have become confused, so have their ages; the husband calls his wife "Mother": she calls him "Father"; both of them call their only son "My friend," while he calls his mother "Darling." He has no word at all for his father, since he stopped addressing him when he was five years old; he never speaks *to* him, never speaks *of* him in his presence, and if he is not there, he uses the plain personal pronoun, the mere monosyllable "Him."

Often, if they both turned their backs upon each other, while one of them was leaving the room, the father would look behind him and find that the son was staring back at him. The son would feel that his father was giving him a piercing look which foreboded something. The father would feel that his son's glance was the look of a person with a gleaming scalpel hidden in his hand. Then the interchanged looks would turn into the embarrassed, apologetic smiles of men whose ruses have been detected; then the smiles, in their turn would change into two looks of understanding, love and esteem: the whole incident would take only a brief moment—and revealed that the family was close-knit, and shared a distinctive feature: every one of them was tender, soft, hypersensitive, as a result of having disengaged himself from others.

LIFE WITHOUT A programme. No wonder the parents showed no surprise, no objection, no regret, when the son broke off his studies at the Faculty of Commerce, after spending a year there which had started out for him with no anxieties or fixed dislikes, but left him with a burning hatred of money and of book-keeping: whenever he swore now, he spat out a figure. They did not react any more strongly when he broke off his study of literature after devoting another year to that: he found that the standards of his mind and his language had been depraved, and that he was taking to a fatuous prattle. He followed this with a year spent idling at home: this fundamentally altered his life, for when it was over, he had altered his attitude. He found himself entering the Faculty of Law, and applied himself to his studies there, passing his examinations every year, though he was placed every time at the bottom of the list. His mind found rest in his studies there: he settled into them, and came within a year of graduation. He liked the way that the Law cut itself off so totally from the ordinances of nature, with their confusion, their contradictions, their claim that injustice was sometimes true justice in disguise, their lack of any final settlement—or, at the most, their postponing of it until the whole world lay in ruins. The Law has invented for itself a self-supporting logic which looks beautiful on paper, distinguished by ingenious subdivisions and sequences, and swift to take effect; as though it has demolished the structure of life, and has turned the rubble into numbered and catalogued matrixes with which it has built its own stronghold. A judge does not pronounce judgment by drawing upon his knowledge of truth—he relies upon paper—for Paper is clearer than Truth. A judge will reject any truth, as easily as a lie, unless it is supported by juridically-admissible evidence which has not been shown to be spurious. He gives vice clearly defined limits; while virtue becomes a vague notion which is not taken into account at all: the judge imposes his penalty upon the adulterous husband, but does not grant a reward to a husband who remains faithful to his wife after their honeymoon is over.

With all this, the virtue of the law is that it

relieves mankind by converting the world of the spirit into logical argumentation where there is no distinction between knowledge and ignorance, between freewill and the determined: it has dropped the word *fate* from the vocabulary of man, and in so doing it has at the same time dropped the word *pity*. No matter, for such is the logical sequence of arguments which the law follows; and however many injustices it may involve, a logical sequence of arguments is to be preferred to a just law which has no discernible logical structure. Forensic logic is so different from the logic of nature's ordinances, that little by little, the young man lost the sense of there being any distinction between virtue and vice. A beggar, who always receives and never gives, withdraws from the bustle of life, lies down on the pavement in front of a mosque, and lays his chest bare; he gives it up both to sunlight and to swarms of lice: and when the two streams that flow over his breast blend together, he finds a delight which makes him at one and the same time whimper with pain and quiver with pleasure.

DURING THE PERIOD that the young man spent idling at home between his year as a student of literature and the beginning of his law-studies, it was natural that one occupation should present itself as a cure for his torpor—an occupation which, of all others, is the simplest to enter upon, the easiest to continue in, the worthiest, the truest and most sensible—and that is the occupation of a husband. He was a virgin, but was determined that the woman he married should be one who was sexually experienced. He decided to make his choice without any intervention from his parents, to pick for himself the workshop that was going to yield up its products for him. He did not run through the list of his relations and neighbours and acquaintances, but seated in his own home, like a priest anointing an emperor, he stretched out his arm upon the head of a penniless girl, and he uttered the one brief phrase, "This one!" like a child in a toyshop. It filled him with boundless joy to think that he had returned to nature and her ways, and had trampled underfoot all the conventions which men had thought up for the winning of a wife: the pursuit, the cornering of the quarry, the carrying off of the prize, the deed of purchase, the hero's proving his prowess in battle, the courtship, the sleepless pillow and the sighings. Sometimes he smiled to himself because he had surmised by sheer mother-wit, without any direct knowledge of the matter, that the unrealized cause of the misery of modern woman is that she has inherited traits from every one of her ancestresses, and wishes her husband to win her by combining all these devices together and bringing them into play, although she falsely claims that because she is a civilized person, courting is the only method it is necessary to use. Why should he bother himself with all this palaver?

The penniless girl, together with her mother, used to come on visits with her father, who was a tenant on the land owned by the young man's family. They came to town whenever the half-yearly instalments of their rent were due. For a dress, she still wore the old-fashioned *malas* of crinkly dyed silk; on her feet, instead of shoes, she wore slippers. She only revealed the tiniest portion of her face; in the grip of a crushing shyness, she would have buried herself in the ground if she could whenever anyone addressed her. He mentally added up her pink ankles and those parts of her face that he had managed to catch a glimpse of, and decided that it was she who would suit him. A simple, raw girl. Downcast eyes that dared not glance at you. A forehead free of any thought. A body in which the finer points of every part had been distributed in common throughout the whole. Matted hair which you could see would be bewitching once it was washed, and once it had been plaited so that it would hang upon her forehead and cheeks: he would rinse it for her with his own hands, and his tongue would find that the taste of soap could intoxicate as well as wine.

He knew that she had already been married to a relation of hers in their home village. The husband had had a rival who had a feud with him. Maliciously vindictive, he would not let him enjoy his newlywed bride in peace, but lay in wait for him when he was on his way home from the fields, and emptied bullets into him from a home-made rifle that he had bored for himself. A mangled corpse was carried home to the bride: she wiped the wounds with her handkerchief and in this way it became bloodstained for the second time in one week. To the young man, then, she was all that he could have hoped for: an easy path to take, already opened up and smoothed out for him by someone else. In the same way if he had bought an earthenware pot, turned and fired for use, he would have left it for someone else to dirty his fingers and scratch them in lining its inside with oil, so that he could use it for cooking. The girl was a better proposition than such a pot, because she was ready moistened—moist with blood, even if the outer layer of it came from the wounds of her murdered husband.

In order to complete his fancy, the young man set out to furnish the bridal-chamber which he had set aside for himself in his family home, in the style of a peasant of his wife's own class: a rush-mat at the edge of which slippers and wooden clogs were to be taken off and lined up; an iron bedstead with wooden planks stretched across it, and a mosquito-net of pink silk; a wooden chest to store clothes in, painted red and green, a basin and jug for washing. But when the bridal equipment was ready, he was taken by surprise to see her lips draw up and whisper in her mother's ear, after which she turned her face to the wall out of excess of shyness, keeping hold of her mother's hand and tugging at it, to make sure that she did not start saying anything while she was still in the room.

As soon as the young man was alone with his mother-in-law, she told him that what her daughter had whispered to her was, "As I'm marrying a Cairo man, and such a high-class man at that, I'd like to have at least a spring mattress on my bed instead of those planks of wood."

On that spring mattress the young man received the deepest shock of his life; it shook his being, and brought his illusions tottering down; it left him naked in their ruins, nursing the wounds of his bewilderment.

On the wedding-night itself, the raw simple girl turned into a fierce wild beast, the downcast eyes gleamed like the eyes of a pouncing hawk, sending into the darkness of the night a glimmer like the flash of a sword or the sudden flaring-up of a smouldering fire; enough to set a brand ablaze, it was a thing that not the waters of all the sacred rivers flowing together could have quenched; it was a look that rasped his body like a file. The forehead that never gleamed with a single idea now had drawn upon it, in place of the smooth blankness of resignation, the execution order of a Court of Summary Justice that allowed no deferment and no appeal. The delicate, ever-closed lips opened and closed in audible smacks, and never kept the one shape for a single moment: at one instant, it was the circular brink of a volcano; the next, it was the inside of a funnelshaped vortex; next, a long slit like a dagger-wound; spasm succeeded spasm as though her gullet contained a grapnel which was being handled by a merciless grip. The open mouth revealed a set of teeth which gleamed with hunger, and dispelled the surrounding shadows by sending them scattering in alarm. The parts of her body which had pleaded that they had lost their individual attractions by having shared them out in common amongst them all, each retrieved its rights and in addition seized and used as its own the enticements that are proper to a body as one single whole. Even her big toe reared itself up and tried to overreach itself. Her voracity was intensified by an underlying contradiction: the palms of her hands lay flat, resigned, passive, bestowing themselves, her arms were limp, the saliva of her mouth was cool and sweet as honey, and her breathing came like that of an innocent babe.

What was he to do? He came from a family which had never given anything of itself: he wanted a goblet of wine that he could swallow down in one gulp, not one that glued itself to his lips like a leech. He had sought his own pleasure, but before he could take it, he was caught in the grip of a liability. He could only accept a liability that he had undertaken of his own free will; he hated any obligation that was imposed upon him, like a poll-tax or a tribute—it was an invasion of the privacy behind which his self-respect preened itself. His self-respect, which was genuine enough, and true to itself, was a thing he was well satisfied with—so long as it remained insulated; he would allow no one else to scrutinize it; it was mortifying to be put in the balance, even if the opposite dish on the pair of scales contained no more than a mustard seed. If any uninvited hand claimed the right to weigh him, to test him, to assess him, then that hand ought to be lopped off.

Ιn spite of his holding this view, he was too astonished to reach any decision. It was the raw simple girl who did so before he did. She bore with him for a second night; on the third, she gave him a kick and said, "We women from Upper Egypt were made for Upper Egyptian men. I piss on your money and your elegance and your fine words."

And she added, as though a prophetic voice spoke through her, "Find yourself a mummy all daubed with white and black and red: there's thousands of them in this town of yours."

She got up and gathered her few pieces of clothing together. In spite of his astonishment, the young man noticed for the first time the fine bridge of her nose, her long, slender neck, and a pair of firm haunches that the noblest Arab mare would have envied.

In the morning it was she who dragged her mother away by the hand, and glided out gingerly as though she were escaping from a captor who had fallen asleep and who might wake up at any moment; her crinkly *malas* of black silk hung forward, making her look as though she were preparing to run for it the moment she had got past the door. And so her second marriage, also, lasted less than a week. When her mother caught a glistening in her eyes of what she took to be the vestiges of tears, she said to her, "Don't you grieve over him: God will send you better than that. This was your lot, and you had to go through with it."

And the daughter replied to herself, "You're so kind, mother, and such a fool! If I were to cry, it would be for my first husband all over again."

AFTER THAT, THE young man could only satisfy his urges and heal his wound by visits to women who traded in passions; none of them had any rights over him, and he had no liabilities towards any; he was happy to deal in cash purchases and not barter—a primitive method which time and progress have overlaid and buried. He made no distinction at first between any one of these women and another.

But, after some time, he began to spruce himself up, and to search out the ones who attracted purchasers to their wares with the same draw that a lump of sugar has for a swarm of flies. The larger the swarm, and the more completely he was swallowed up in it, the more it pleased him: it made him feel that his face had become a mask. But he did not find the absolute pleasure he had hoped for: even with the ones in briskest demand, he thought he detected some turn of the head, some curl of the lip, some thrust of the arm, which upset his assurance. What he wished for now was a woman whose face would remain frozen in perfect stillness, even if it had to be made of wax, with lips rigid as wood, or fashioned in a mould, a woman who could not move her arms, even if that meant that she would be as cold as ice . . . and where should he find one like that?

NO ONE CAN tell what would have become of him if he had not had a strange illness which kept him in bed for some time. The doctors said that it was a minor infection, a harmless microbe which is present even in the bodies of the fit, where the red corpuscles easily destroy it without artificial aid. His body, however, was unable to resist it, not because of any organic deficiency, but because he had lost his will to resist. Every medicine they gave him was so much lost effort: his physical frame became a field tussled over by the sweetness of life and the putrescence of decay.

It seemed animated by mere clockwork. He was like a breathing creature under whose skin every morsel of flesh had been eaten away by a gangrene, leaving nothing but the look that gleamed out of his eye-socket. The doctors recommended his father to consult a psychologist.

This piece of advice stung the young man to the quick. As soon as the doctors were out of the house, he got up, and went to the bathroom to draw the evil out of himself, and put the past behind him: he washed himself, purified himself, reaffirmed his faith. Freshened-up, his face, when he emerged, wore a look of content, of gentleness. His movements and gestures fell into a harmonious order, and grew unusually calm. As a result of this, in the days that immediately followed, some people looked upon him as dull-witted, although he thought of his mannerisms as the height of elegance, and now paid great attention to his fingernails and necktie, and saw to it that his clothes matched one another. He took to moving with a demureness which suggested a woman's coquettishness, to speaking in a low, nasal tone; there was languor in his eyes; although his tall body now stooped slightly, this did not impair his good looks, but added a touch of deference, and, by setting off his head, even gave him, in some people's eyes, a deceptive air of acumen. In fact, to some, his stoop made him seem cunning and inquisitive—though God knows he was innocent of this.

And so that phase of his life came to a close. He entered the Faculty of Law, where his elegance and his sober bearing drew the notice of his fellow-students. They would hover around him, not knowing quite what attracted them to him: could it be his nails, his lithe fingers, the honey that flowed out of his eyes, or the curious quality in his voice? And yet not one of them advanced his acquaintance with him far enough to become a true friend, to be joined to him in an attachment which would separate them off from the crowd they were in. He did not feel lonely, but was quite at ease: to the honey of his looks he added a sweet-natured smile, which made him into a model of kindness and high-mindedness, in the eyes of the other students: "That," they would say to one another, "is how a really high-born young man behaves."

IT WAS WITHIN a year of his final examinations. He lay on his bed one morning, and glanced out of his window. It was autumn. The Nile had fallen out of its summer stir and back into repose. It had been the liquor of zizyphus fruit coursing down from distant mountains: now it was a muddy brownness as scaly as a fish's skin. Exhausted with its work of fecundating the earth, it withdrew into its burrow to hibernate; losing its prowess, it now suggested, more strongly than anything else could, the ague, the darkness of the lower depths, an enormous heaviness. The fields had put well behind them the days when they had been dry and naked, with a cracked skin; now they wore a mantle of blossoms, and offered its nectar to the bees and the grazing herds. A fresh breeze from a blue sky annihilated all malignancy. Lying on his bed, he could see the sky and watch a train of maiden clouds, brightly decked out and freshly combed, making fun of earth-dwellers by mimicking some of the things which can be seen in their lives. An unseen hand had poured out over the world a flood of happiness. A bird flew into view with a broad span of black wings, crying out as it bathed in the sunlight. It was a plover: the cry of that bird, according to his mother, presaged the arrival of a traveller. The bird's call only lasted a brief time, but in those moments were expelled from man all his chains and fetters, his captivity and fears, his uncertainties, delusions, and pollutions, and he became a pure and innocent being, who enjoyed a freedom that had no bounds, fit only for an angel or a fiend. This freedom floated down into the heart of the young man with a tremor. It vexed him that it should be so vigorous, and that it should not make itself fully plain to the limited vision of one who was a cross between angel and fiend.

Well, then, he had no need of it. He turned his face to
the wall. An appalling weariness seeped into him, and took
over the whole of his being: it tinged his gullet with the
bitterness of wormwood, it ran in his veins where his
blood had run before; his body now sweated it out, his
eyelashes were now spun out of it, and the dirt between
his toes was now made of it.

HE DID NOT go out that day until later than his usual
time. As he stepped out of his doorway, his eyes fell upon
the small shop which stood opposite. It had lain empty for
many months. Now, he saw that it had been opened up: a
man upon a ladder was hanging up a board which read
"Undertaker for Whole of Imamein District." His heart
sank. Was it a mere chance that one and the same morning
had brought him this world-weariness, and had seen the
arrival of this servant of death? Could one of the two be
the traveller whose arrival the plover had heralded? Or were
events contrived according to some set plan, working out a
pre-arranged purpose?

He saw the undertaker's apprentice—for that is what he took him to be—urging the workman on the ladder to hurry, with the result that the man misjudged the centre of the rope as he was attaching it to its nail. As soon as the workman had come down off the ladder, the apprentice brought out a coffin and hung it up on one flap of the door. He felt that there was someone looking at him, and he looked up: the two glances met, and the appearance of the apprentice registered itself in the young man's mind in a clear-cut image, standing out from the rest of things, as though he were shining a spotlight onto him through some gaping hole in his own body. He saw a youngish man, with a body bulging like cotton in a hooped bale; stunted in height, with stumpy arms and bulky hands, a low forehead and narrow-slit eyes; his piercing look had the tinselly gleam of sequins, the whites of his eyes setting off a flame-coloured glitter which spoke of cunning and rancour, of a disturbed and malicious spirit and the hunger of an animal: a creature determined to kill a rival with a glance would wear a look like this one. The young man was sure that he had seen this figure before . . . But where? He could not tell. Until he remembered that it had been in a book he had read about the theories of Darwin. His look, too; that was the look in his own father's eyes when the time had come for a sniff of cocaine or a shot of opium.

As he turned away, he saw that the apprentice was smiling at him, and raising his hand to his forehead in a friendly greeting. He walked away, knowing for certain that he would be coming back to him.

THE FRIENDSHIP BETWEEN them grew. The young man now took up the habit of spending his evenings sitting in front of the shop with the undertaker's apprentice. At first he used to come to him fully dressed in his suit and shoes; but after some time he gave this up, and saw no reason why he should not come out in slippers, and in the *gallabiyya* which he wore indoors. The apprentice's conversation was all about his work, its seasonal fluctuations, the glories it had known in the past, its pleasures and pains, its ritual and artistry, and the little tricks of his trade. One day he said to the young man:

"You're so interested in everything I say about it—you ask so many questions—you want to know so much; why don't you come with me next time we're sent for? I can say you're one of our boys. No one will be any the wiser."

In his great boredom, he accepted the offer, and went indoors.

HE HAD NEVER seen a dead body before. They turned into a narrow, muddy alleyway, towards a house that stood shrouded in silence. When the people in the house noticed them, the building burst out in shrieks, wailings, the striking of cheeks in lamentation, and the pounding of feet upon the flat housetop; the house was behaving like a sick woman at an exorcism, when she hears the drumming of the exorcists starting up. At first, he was dumbfounded, and almost forgot himself so far as to clap his hands over his ears. Then he found himself threading his way through a crowd of small boys who were celebrating the obsequies with jollification: the discrepancy between the sounds and the boys' faces calmed him down. They clambered up a narrow staircase which the apprentice measured with his eyes, to estimate whether it was broad enough for the coffin. When they were inside the flat, the screaming and wailing, and the striking of cheeks, flared up once again, but in the middle of the uproar, his ears were able to distinguish the hiss of a primus stove, and he realized that they had not forgotten to put some water on the boil for the laying-out. Surrounded by tearful women in black headveils, he nevertheless had the impression that they were receiving him as they would receive a first-aid man. In fact, one old woman patted him on the back and said:

"Come on, sonny; you'll be wanting to get down to your work—and may God send you down His blessings."

He understood now how men of this profession could take a pride in their work and be contented with themselves. The apprentice drew him by the hand into a room where a corpse lay upon a mattress on the ground. He asked him to help carry the body to the bathroom, where the laying-out table, with a can of water upon the primus stove, had been placed, complete with jug and bowl, a loofah, and a piece of soap in readiness. But some of the members of the family were unwilling to allow a strange hand to touch the body until it was absolutely unavoidable, and so it was they themselves who carried it in on to the table: the apprentice then turned them out of the bathroom, allowing only one of them, an old man, to remain there, reciting verses from the Koranic *Sura* of *Yassin*—for a laying-out is not canonical unless witness is present.

With the deft hand of a pastry cook tossing a pancake, the undertaker's apprentice flung the white sheet off the corpse, so that it seemed to the young man like the wing of some legendary bird flapping above and around him, trying to touch him. Now that the cover had been removed, he stood for the first time face to face with a dead person.

Something that lies outside the division of things into three kingdoms, and forces on to you a new classification into two kingdoms that know no third: into corpses and non-corpses. A solid thing, and yet made of soft flesh, in the shape of a human being, and yet not human—and not animal either, or "mineral." What affected him most was that when he looked at it, he could not tell whether he was confronted by a resignation which had reached the point of torment, or a torment carried so far that it passed into resignation. Was this dead body an arrested shriek, or was it the echo of a paean of praise? Was it a cry of jubilation which meant "I am your servant, o my beloved!"? Or was it a stifling of a moan which tried to say, "Enough, o Lord of mine!"? Neither. It was simply nothing. And this thing which was no thing was in the form of a human being, but this was not a face that could be averted, this was not a mouth that would screw up in disdain, these were not arms that would push one away.

The young man's fear dissolved, and he fell to washing the corpse, gently, with a pitifulness that made the undertaker's apprentice lose his patience.

"Come on," he cried, "Hurry up—before they hide the counterpane from us."

IT NOW BECAME his habit to come down to the shop every day in *gallabiyya* and slippers; he insisted on accompanying the apprentice whenever he was sent for—in fact he would hurry to the address before the other did. A day that passed without a body seemed dull and colourless. He worked with the ardour of a passionate craftman. His hands were eager to finger the merchandise all over. At first sight, all corpses may look much the same, but to the contemplative lover every one is different: Does it have open palms or clenched fists? Are the legs outstretched? Or are the knees bent, so that the legs are raised up stiffly towards the breast, like those of a newborn child, and the undertaker's apprentice has to press down upon them with all his weight in order to get the body into the coffin, and he sometimes wishes he had a hammer or a saw with him? A dwarf as heavy as lead. A giant as light as a feather. A corpse which is nothing more than rotting flesh upon decaying bones. Another which is a filled-out balloon. A face convulsed in fear. A face in repose, as though it were enjoying the calmest of rests.

The undertaker's apprentice realized that the young man could no longer leave him: he saw his smile becoming sweeter and gentler, and his eyes more langorous, while his body grew more softly pliable. When he sat with the young man now, he would sidle up right next to him, put his arm round his shoulders and then let it drop round his waist. Whenever he spoke to him it would be in a whisper during which he held his mouth to the young man's ear. When he thought that his dish was cooked, he whispered one day:

"If you don't know what to do with yourself, just put yourself in my hands. Come on. Don't be standoffish. Don't be afraid. It's quite dark on the inside of the shop. And there's a big coffin there that'll take the two of us."

The young man brushed off these assaults, but he never complained or showed any anger: his thoughts were wandering in the dream kingdom of the grave.

THE UNDERTAKER'S APPRENTICE resorted to a ruse which he had picked up from others of his kind. When the young man joined him on the day when he put it into operation, he made a point of keeping his distance, as though he had given up hope, or had come to his senses. He gave him no particular attention, but fell to making general reflexions, cursing the times and regretting the old days. When he felt that the young man had been lulled into lowering his guard, he broke off his chatter and exclaimed that he had suddenly remembered a piece of news of prime importance.

"Have you heard? That woman who's our opposite number in the trade tells us that this blessed morning she's had the biggest day's takings that she's ever made in the trade and that she's ever likely to make in it to the end of her life. She was sent for to lay out a bride. Comes of a rich lot and was to have got married the next day. Her white dress was hanging up ready for her. The wedding attendant turned up and went into the bathroom with her to get her spruced up. She's hardly scrubbed her down, and she's just got up from beside the washstand to spray a bottle of scent over her, when she holds her hand to her heart and gives one sigh—and she's gone. They had music at the funeral, and they've strewn the ground over her grave with henna. And what's more, they insisted that she should have her wedding dress on, and her head wreathed in jasmine."

A bride in her first youth, bathed twice over and lying in her wedding-gown with flowers strewn over her. And tonight a new moon.

"Fair or dark?" the young man asked with a catch in his throat.

"Dark. They say she may have come from Upper Egypt."

When he heard that, he jumped up and seized the undertaker's apprentice by the collar.

"Show me the way to her grave," he pleaded hoarsely.

And the man whispered back:

"On condition that you won't refuse, this time. On condition that you'll let me."

Two shadowy figures hurried off in the dark—a ravenous animal which would have swallowed gravel, and a broken, putrescent spirit from whom God had withdrawn His mercy.

ONE MORNING A message comes to the family from the hospital: their man of mark can no longer cut any figure in this world. His bed is empty, and waiting for a new occupant.

Translated by Mahmoud Manzalaoui; revised by Leonard Knight and Lewis Hall.

Michael Palin

CAIRO

Sunday morning in Cairo.

I wake with a greater than usual feeling of sensory dislocation. Where am I and what is the horrendous noise? Most of it can be attributed to my air-conditioning unit which changed gear during the night with a splintering crack that sounded as if someone were trying to batter the door down.

Michael Palin was one of the cofounders of the BBC Television series "Monty Python's Flying Circus." He has since moved on to more respectable ventures, including two documentaries of his travels around the world. This is from the book version of his first trip, Around the World in 80 Days.

I silence the air conditioner and throw open the windows only to find there's even more noise outside. I now know why they had laughed at me in reception when I'd asked for a quiet room.

"In *Cairo!*"

I suppose it's sheer weight of numbers. There are over 10 million people living in Greater Cairo and a further million or more unrecorded refugees and squatters—many of them living in the eerily beautiful City of the Dead, a huge and ancient cemetery. I passed by it with fascination, but on enquiry found that cameras are not allowed inside, so, with a day to kill before my next boat connection from Suez, Passepartout and I take up the invitation of a man I met in the bar last night to visit an Egyptian movie set. Crossing the Nile by the Tahir bridge I have my first sight of the more prosperous side of the metropolis. Hilton, Sheraton and Meridien Hotels, skyscraper office blocks. From here Cairo could be anywhere in the world and I'm glad to be at the eccentric Windsor, in the as yet unsmoothed heart of the city.

The film is a political thriller called *Inar Gahined* ("Hellfire") and it's being shot in a Safeway supermarket in the tidy, tree-shaded Zamalek area. Foreign diplomats live here, so it's well tended, well guarded, and dotted with twee boutiques with names like "Mix 'n Match" and "Genuine."

It transpires that my contact is Egypt's leading lighting cameraman and I'm treated royally, meeting the stars and, without any audition, being given the part of Third Shopper In China Department. My six steps to the left as the gang pass by are executed so successfully that I am up-graded to the more demanding Man In Lift. The terrorists have a gritty scene here in which their recriminations are cut short by the arrival of the elevator, whose doors slide open to reveal yours truly. I'm not quite sure what I'm doing but I stare hard at the gang leader as I walk past him and he seems very pleased.

I talk to him afterwards. His real name is Noor-el-Sherif and he is very big in Egypt—where they make over sixty films a year. He admits only about six of these are any good and blames much of the blandness on the censorship that is necessary to make pictures saleable in the rest of the Arab world. I ask him what sort of things they censor.

"Sex, politics, religion . . . " he replies gloomily. "That's all."

HAVING ARRIVED IN Egypt six hundred years too late to see one of the Seven Wonders of the World—the Pharos lighthouse—I felt I couldn't leave without seeing one that still exists—the Pyramids. I had always presumed they were in the middle of nowhere, marooned in the desert. In fact they are within five minutes' walk of apartment blocks in the suburb of Giza. My first view of them is from a traffic jam on Pyramids Road. The 4600-year-old apex of the Great Pyramid pokes up from behind a block of flats. My first full-frontal view of the Pyramids provokes an heretical comparison with the slag-heaps which used to litter the South Yorkshire countryside where I grew up. They had the same solid bulk, shape and immovable presence. Once free of the straggling suburb we are straightaway in desert. There's no transition through savannah and scrubland, like in the geography books. The city ends, the desert begins, and it goes on until you reach Morocco. The dustiness of Cairo is explained. Every time a wind blows it dumps thousands of tons of desert on the city.

Closer now to the Pyramids and they are awesome. The blocks of sandstone at their base are twice as high as the small children playing around them. The structures rise serene and powerful above us, preserving an unmoving dignity, like great beasts surrounded by insects. Coaches ferry out an endless stream of human insects, deposit them at a tightly packed vantage point where they are assailed by camel-mongers, postcard salesmen, purveyors of trinkets and all the other free market forces which have ripped off tourists at this very spot for hundreds, if not thousands, of years.

They have their patter well worked out, and very bizarre it sounds in the middle of the desert:

"You from Yorkshire? . . . I am friend of Yorkshire!"

"You are English? Tally-ho!"

"What is your name?"

"Michael."

"My camel's name is Michael!"

So it is that I find myself on a camel called Michael (or Ron or Julian or Nigel or Dwayne or Sheri-Anne) being flung skywards into the air as the creature raises itself on its forelegs. It looks and feels grossly unsafe, as it totters into the desert with me clinging on for dear life and feeling ridiculously conspicuous in an Arab head-dress which the camel-owner, who I think is called Michael as well, has insisted I wear: "Now you will be like Lawrence of Arabia!"

Behind me hot white people from all over the wealthy West are being given similar treatment. Every time they raise a camera to the Pyramids an Arab stands in front of it. The tourist adjusts his shot, the Arab follows. The air is full of the angry din of protest and dissension. This din is beginning to fade now as Michael, Michael and Michael wander further into the desert. In silence and sunset the Pyramids take on a potent, talismanic quality.

Lawrence of Arabia

HOME LETTERS

MILITARY INTELLIGENCE OFFICE, CAIRO
16.6.15

Well, here's another week gone, & nothing has happened or is happening, except an occasional Turkish feint on the canal: it's very hot here, with a Khamsin blowing so that we

---

Lawrence of Arabia, a.k.a. T.E. Lawrence, made his name by leading an Arab rebellion against the Turks during World War I. As an innovative archaeologist, glorious war hero, and distinguished author, Lawrence became a legend—throughout the Mideast, and thanks to the movies, throughout America. After the war, he retired to private life, writing and translating Homer's Odyssey.

have to keep all doors and windows shut. The shade temperature outside the office is 115° just now. Yesterday was 112°, but it cools down to 95° or 100° at night; it has gone up to 117° now: it must really be rather like the Persian Gulf, and yet it doesn't feel at all oppressive.

We are very busy just now. I don't really know what with: there is a lot of telegraphing to do, in cipher, which takes a long time—and we have other work, & besides I have 6 maps in hand being drawn.

Wainwright passed through yesterday, going to England. He had been digging in Egypt for some weeks.

Tell Arnie to get out Collignon's book on Greek sculpture. There is a beautiful frontispiece of a head in the Louvre.

—*T.E.L.*

CAIRO, SAVOY HOTEL

21.2.16

Post is going tomorrow, so I'm going to write now. Nothing to say, as usual. Newcombe is back in Cairo for a few days; he *may* be going back to the W.O. for a few days, though I shouldn't think so. He will probably be made a Colonel shortly. We are changing office tonight, so that everything is in a royal disorder. Each time we change we get more and more rooms: here in the Savoy Hotel, which is Headquarters at present, we now have 15 rooms, not counting little rooms. I have now got quite a decent room to myself, and have decorated it with a map of the Caucasus about 15 feet long (the largest map I have ever seen) one of Syria, about 12 feet high, and the beginnings of one on Egypt, bigger than either of these. It is rather amusing work publishing and drawing maps. We are up to 1,000,000 now, actual sheets, (mostly Gallipoli) of a total of about 600 different maps. The Egyptian Government handed over its Survey Department to us—or rather Dowson, Director General of Surveys, handed it over to us, and the Government agreed—so that there are about 1,000 workmen and a very large plant (second only to Southampton) at our disposal. The cost has not been what one would expect: paper etc. about £28,000: and expenses of staff etc. about £75,000. Egypt pays the second, War Office the first. There is a very great deal in hand just now. I wish I could send Arnie some of them. However you got the Gallipoli, which was a very pretty map. I have a lovely little 500,000 of the Turkish Empire in hand just now. It will take about six months to do. Also an Arabia (two months) which will be an important thing. I wish there was some news to tell you: there is heaps as a matter of fact just now, but it is not for publication. We seem to be fixed for ever in Cairo: all efforts now are directed to organizing the office so that it continues after the War on its present scale. They will have to find a substitute for me! We have got a little man called Deedes in our office now: he is an ex-Turkish Gendarmerie instructor, captain in the English Army, and a very excellent man. I like him best of the bunch. I'm going to bed now.   — N.

ARAB BUREAU, SAVOY HOTEL, CAIRO

25.2.17

Back in Cairo again for a few days—till the 28th to be exact. One does run about on this show! But as a matter of fact I have only come up to get some mules, and a wireless set, and a few such-like things.

Affairs are going a little slower than I had hoped, but there has been no suspicion of a set-back, and we are all well contented. I enclose a few photographs—as long as they are not published there is no harm in showing them to anyone. I have a lot more, but they have not been printed yet. They will give you an idea of the sort of country (in the oases) and the sort of people we have to do with. It is of course by far the most wonderful time I have had. I don't know what to write about! What we will do when I get back I don't know exactly—and cannot say any how. Cairo is looking very gay, and everybody dances & goes to races as usual or more so—but after all, there is not, and never has been, war in Egypt.

The weather here is fresh—and in Wejh warmish.

Tell Arnie that I think his drawings try after ease too quickly. There is no point in making lines because other people do. The way is to look at a thing long enough, & try & make up your mind which way you have to twist your point to show up its shape in black and white. It will take a long time to do a drawing, but you do get a certain amount of thought and direction into it—not very much, I'm afraid, unless you are an artist, and born to it. After you have thought out how to do it, then you can get easy, & put polish on. Modelling is better, because there you show things as they really are, instead of recording solids in flat. I don't like relief, for that reason, unless it is half-round, and shows only half the object—otherwise it seems to me only a meretricious sketching. The greatest works I can remember are the battered heads of Skopas, the torso of Poseidon from the Parthenon, and some of the more fluid heads, like the Collignon athlete, Hypnos, etc. Above all, those two wonderful heads.

I got the headcloth safely, about a week ago, in

Wejh, together with news that Bob had gone to France. As a matter of fact, you know, he will be rather glad afterwards that he has been . . . and as it will be easier work, and healthier than his hospital work in London. I do not think that you have much cause to regret. Many thanks for the headcloth.

I wrote to C. B. Young, and asked him to send me Will's Pindar.

I have now been made Captain and Staff Captain again, which is amusing. It doesn't make any difference of course really, as I am never in uniform in Arabia, and nobody cares a straw what rank I hold, except that I am of Sherif Feisul's household. Can't think of anything else to say, as have become a monomaniac about the job in hand, and have no interest of recollections except Arabian politics just now! It's amusing to think that this will suddenly come to an end one day, and I take up other work.

— *N.*

CAIRO

28.2.17

Dear Arnie

Herewith a few 1/8 piastre Hejaz stamps—a new denomination just going to be issued. The perforation I think better than the old style, and I like the design. What do you think? Inform me if there are any other values of which you want more. Those published are I P.T. 1/2, 1/4, 1/8 P.T. Blue, Red, Green and Orange. Also tax stamps, but I don't suppose you care about them. A 2 P.T. is under weigh. It has an arch-&-grill design, and I like it.

Just off again.

— *N.*